lonely planet

AF215342

POCKET
VIENNA

Becki Enright

Contents

Top: Crown Jewels at the Kaiserliche
Schatzkammer (p38)
Bottom: Spanische Hofreitschule (p39)

Plan Your Trip — 4

Explore Vienna 33

Vienna Toolkit 141

FROM TOP LEFT: JULIA MOUNTAIN PHOTO/SHUTTERSTOCK, PETER RIGAUD

★ Top Experiences

★ Worth a Trip

The Journey Begins Here

What's not to love about a city steeped in thousands of years of history, with Roman ruins, medieval foundations and baroque streetscapes, grand imperial palaces and masterpiece art museums, chandelier-lit *Kaffeehäuser* (coffee houses) and wood-panelled *Beisln* (bistro pubs). But know that Vienna is quite the chameleon. Beyond the splendour of Habsburg heritage, this is a modern metropolis refashioned, melding its heady historic sites with bohemian *Bezirke* (districts), and its time-honoured traditions with cutting-edge contemporary culture. A city of subtly woven eras and unhurried revival, Vienna modestly and slowly unfurls; despite taking time, pack your curiosity.

Becki Enright
@bordersofadventure
Becki is an award-winning travel writer and guide-book author. She writes extensively about Vienna, the city she has called home for the past 10 years.

Stephansdom, Stephansplatz (p54)
ALEXANDER SPATARI/GETTY IMAGES

Masterpiece Museum Experiences

A world-class centre for the arts, many of Vienna's remarkable collections date back to the Habsburgs, whose extraordinary cache of paintings, sculptures and curiosities were displayed in the palaces now home to grand museums and galleries.

Lose yourself in the **Kunsthistorisches Museum** (pictured above), packed with Egyptian, Greek and Roman antiquities, peculiar and rare objects, and European old masters paintings. (p46)

Behold the most important displays of Austrian early Modernism and the world's most comprehensive Egon Schiele collection in the MuseumsQuartier's white art hulk **Leopold Museum**. (p114)

Roam the halls of the art trove **Oberes Belvedere** (Upper Belvedere), showcasing Austrian pieces from the Middle Ages to the present day and the world's largest collection of Gustav Klimt's works. (p86)

Browse the history of graphic art and master sketcher works, including Monet, Picasso and Dürer, and wander the luxurious Habsburg State Rooms of former royal palace, **Albertina** (pictured above). (p42)

Right: Oberes Belvedere (p86)

THE BEST

Coffee House Culture Experiences

Vienna's first coffee house opened in 1683, a legacy granted UNESCO Intangible Cultural Heritage in 2011. In the Innere Stadt's cafes – whether poster-plastered, Art Nouveau or chandelier-lit – locals gather in the tradition of coffee, cake and conversation.

Join the queue for 1876 **Café Central**, (pictured above) which has a decadent in-house patisserie and second-to-none vaulted, marble and gilded interior. (p65)

Pause in **Café Prückel**, the 1903 Art Nouveau style icon of the Ringstrasse's original cafes serving homemade sweet dumplings. (p65)

Hibernate in 1939 **Café Hawelka**, a late-night bohemian institution known for its jam-filled *Buchteln* (sweet rolls). (p65)

Experience quintessential Vienna in the red-upholstered grandeur of **Café Sacher** (pictured above), where the Original *Sacher Torte* is always in the house. (p65)

Choose rococo-regency salon cafe **Demel** for *Kaiserschmarrn* (pancake pieces), though its *Demel-Sacher-Torte* compares with the Sacher original. (p65)

Shoot a game of billiards while in the chandeliered 1880 **Café Sperl**, serving a secret recipe chocolate, vanilla and almond *Sperl Torte*. (p108)

Right: Demel (p65)

FROM LEFT: ANDREI ANTIPOV/SHUTTERSTOCK, HOTEL SACHER WIEN, VOLKER VORNEHM/SHUTTERSTOCK

KIEVVICTOR/SHUTTERSTOCK

Secession building (p63)

Architecture Experiences

Vienna's architectural icons meld the medieval gothic and imperial baroque and rococo with the Renaissance revival and Neoclassical simplicity of the Ringstrasse era and the flourishing Secessionist *Jugendstil* (Art Nouveau) and Modernist movements.

Stand before soaring **Stephansdom**, dominating Vienna's historic centre in Gothic glory; its sky-poking south tower reaches 136.4m high. (p44)

Tour the medieval castle turned baroque bastion of the **Hofburg**, the imperial home and treasure coffer for over 600 years. (p38)

Saunter through the exuberant rococo imperial summer home **Schloss Schönbrunn**, the epitome of baroque architectural and horticultural beauty. (p130)

Step into the dual complex baroque palace **Belvedere**, home of Habsburg military general Prince Eugene of Savoy. (p86)

Circuit Vienna's iconic Historicism-style buildings on the **Ringstrasse** including the university, city hall, opera and parliament. (p56)

See the new age of *Jugendstil* design at the **Secession** building – the founding home of the avant-garde Viennese art movement. (p63)

THE BEST
Music Experiences

Classical music is in Vienna's DNA. Centuries on, live performances of composing geniuses resound daily in grand halls while pop, rock and jazz also have a lively home here, with modern venues staging global artists.

Watch a performance in the world capital of opera, the renowned **Wiener Staatsoper** (pictured above), with the largest repertoire and daily rotating performances. (p57)

Revel in live and late-night music venues on the **Gürtel** road's half-mile strip of railway-arch bars. (p121)

Choose a performance from the **Konzerthaus** seasonal catalogue of 750 events covering classical, jazz, pop and world music. (p94)

Feel the beats of basement jazz and music club **Porgy & Bess**, which hosts European and international talent. (p63)

Choose edgy venue **Arena Wien** for punk, rock, metal and alternative music acts on the site of a former slaughterhouse. (p94)

Attend a traditional concert in the Goldener Saal (Golden Hall) at the prestigious **Musikverein** (pictured above), home of the Wiener Philharmoniker. (p61)

THE BEST

Modern Gallery Experiences

The city's rich art legacy may run centuries deep, but it's complemented by a thriving contemporary showcase. Find all manner of modern, expressive and boundary-pushing visual works across a host of unique galleries.

Find Classical Modernism, experiential avant-garde and radical Vienna Actionism exhibits in the MuseumsQuartier's **mumok**. (p114)

Visit the city's newer gallery, **Albertina Modern**, with postwar contemporary works of Austrian artists, alongside international greats. (p63)

Mix it up in the steel-glass Modernist box gallery and sculpture garden of

Belvedere 21, an experimental arm of its palatial namesake. (p91)

Walk through the permanent gallery of artist and eco-warrior Friedensreich Hundertwasser at the **KunstHausWien**. (p94)

See the **Secession** showpiece, Klimt's *Beethoven Frieze*, before browsing the socially expressive contemporary exhibitions in its smaller halls. (p63)

Belvedere 21 (p91)

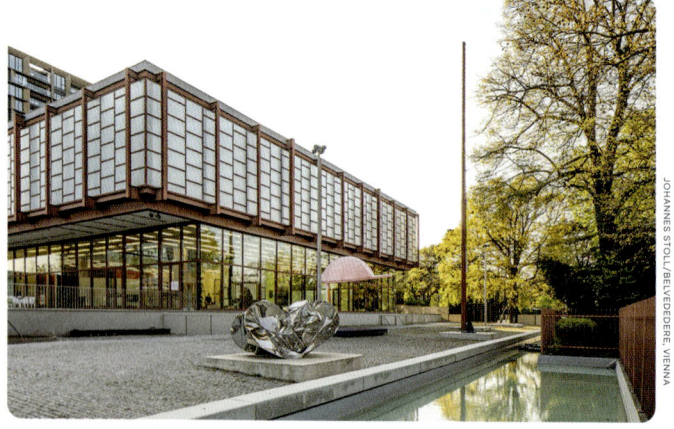

JOHANNES STOLL/BELVEDERE, VIENNA

12

THE BEST

Traditional Culinary Experiences

Traditional *Wiener Küche* (Viennese cuisine) is rooted in imperial tastes. From *Beisln* (bistro pubs), *Würstelstände* (sausage stands) and *Heurigen* (wine taverns) to contemporary joints pushing in new directions, dining here is a serving of the city's history.

Taste Vienna's signature *Wiener Schnitzel* (fried, breadcrumbed veal cutlet; pictured above), perfected in the open kitchen at **Meissl & Schadn**. (p64)

Tuck into Emperor Franz Joseph's favourite *Tafelspitz* (boiled beef served with roasted potatoes, vegetables and horseradish sauce) at **Plachutta Stammhaus Hietzing**. (p132)

Try the hearty, Hungarian origin *Gulasch* (paprika-spiced meat stew)

at Naschmarkt's oldest *Beisl* (bistro pub), **Zur eisernen Zeit**. (p108)

Devour the late-night snack staple, *Käsekrainer* (sausage filled with tiny cubes of cheese), at Vienna's oldest **Würstelstand LEO**. (p124)

Book a table with a Stadtpark view at **Meierei im Stadtpark** (pictured above) for a fine dining taste of contemporary Austrian cuisine and speciality cheese. (p95)

THE BEST

Christmas Market Experiences

Twinkling cobblestoned lanes, glittering historic squares, glimmering palace grounds and park-set Christmas villages – Vienna is at its most enchanting during the Advent season with its 20 or more wonder-filled Wiener Christkindlmärkte.

Start big at the **Rathausplatz** market's 120 huts, vintage carousel, tree light displays and mega ice rink (pictured above), with the theme Christmas Dream. (p63)

Wander the romantic cobbled lanes of **Spittelberg**, an idyllic walk through 100 eco-focused artisan booths and bio food stands. (p119)

Skate the traditional ice rink and stroll through 90 regional maker booths to against the impressive imperial backdrop of **Schloss Schönbrunn**. (p130)

Get creative at **Karlsplatz Art Advent** (pictured above), a showcase of handpicked crafters, visual arts makers and live music acts. (p103)

Eat and drink your way around Austrian federal state-themed huts at the University Campus **Weihnachtsdorf Altes AKH**. (p123)

Head lakeside at **Schloss Belvedere**, the baroque stage for a small, stately market, featuring over 40 unique, traditional gift stalls. (p86)

Right: Schloss Belvedere (p86)

LAMÉE ROOFTOP

Lamée Rooftop Bar (p66)

THE BEST
Drinking Experiences

In a city where heritage intertwines with the cutting edge, the drinking scene is no exception, spanning beer gardens and microbreweries, cocktail lounges and speakeasies, rooftop hangouts and wine bars.

Enjoy draft Budweiser Budvar (lager), Zwickl (unfiltered), Dunkel (dark) beer and more at **Schweizerhaus**, Prater's traditional beer garden since 1766. (p73)

Try European microbrewery, small-batch and experimental flavour pours at the indy **Ammutsøn Craft Beer Dive**. (p109)

Continue the exploration into the historic centre's timeless style with a cocktail at the creative **Dino's Apothecary Bar**. (p66)

Find the inner district secret bars, like the floral-clad, Art Deco booth **Fitzcarraldo**, hidden behind a vending machine. (p123)

Sip at hotel heights with a prime view of Stephansdom at the chic **Lamée Rooftop Bar**. (p66)

Taste European vintage, fine and rare wines by the glass at hip **Pub Klemo Weinbar**. (p109)

Best for Kids

See pandas, polar bears, tigers, rhinos, capybaras and more while learning about international conservation breeding programmes at the world's oldest zoo, **Tiergarten Schönbrunn** (p134).

Take a sensory journey through the **Haus der Musik** (p62) with multimedia symphony-filled rooms, a sound science laboratory and an entertaining Virtual Conductor experience.

Dress up as princes and princesses and see how the imperial children lived at the **Kindermuseum Schönbrunn** (p134) and watch majestic puppet performances at the **Marionettentheatre** (p134).

Browse billions of years of history at the **Naturhistorisches Museum** (p50) with minerals and meteorites, dinosaur bones (and an animatronic replica) and a fascinating anthropology section.

Get hands-on with arts, crafts and animation studios, themed exhibition stages and an ocean-themed toddler playground at the MuseumsQuartier's **Zoom Museum** (p117).

Best for Free

Visit the artefact-packed **Wien Museum** (p100) which chronicles the urban history of Vienna through ancient eras and art movements, wartime changes and cultural transformations.

Discover that it's not always about the interiors on a saunter through the palace gardens of terraced **Belvedere** (p89), folly-filled **Schönbrunn** (p133) and the lawns of **Hofburg** (p43) – without spending a cent.

Roam the ringed historic **Innere Stadt** (p35) and find an open-air museum of Roman ruins, medieval townhouses, grand palaces and a free-to-glimpse cathedral interior.

Find no-charge entry beach bars and recreational hangouts as well as a free summer music festival on the 21km-long isle, **Donauinsel** (Danube Island; p78).

See the Spanish Riding School's resident Lipizzaner horses resting in the **Stallburg** (Stable Palace) or relaxing early morning in the **Burggarten** (p42) when they aren't performing.

Perfect Days

From the ruins of Roman Vindobona to its rise as a cultural bastion of Europe, countless experiences encapsulate Vienna's millennia of history. Take a break at a traditional coffee house, waterside hangout or trendsetting locale.

Griechenbeisl (p64)

DAY ONE

Only Have One Day?

MORNING

Begin in the historic centre, at the soaring **Stephansdom** (p44). Wander between cobblestoned lanes and courtyards, palace grounds and parks, before admiring the most important buildings on the **Ringstrasse** (p56).

AFTERNOON

Take a break in a Viennese coffee house. Cafés **Prückel**, **Schwarzenberg** and **Landtmann** (pictured above; p65) are the last remaining of the ring road's original 27 cafes. Then marvel at the majestic **Hofburg** (p38), starting with the **Kaiserappartements** (Imperial Apartments; p38).

EVENING

Feast at **Figlmüller** (p64), the original home of the schnitzel, or dine in **Griechenbeisl** (p64), the city's oldest restaurant. Catch a performance at the **Wiener Staatsoper** (Vienna State Opera; p57) or have a nightcap in the 1908 Art Deco **Loos American Bar** (p66).

DAY TWO   DAY THREE

A Weekend Trip

MORNING

Beat the crowds and tour the imperial
family's summer residence, **Schloss
Schönbrunn** (p130), when it opens,
ending with a saunter through
its gardens. Or visit **Belvedere**
(p86), the princely palace turned
art museum and home to Gustav
Klimt's *Der Kuss* (The Kiss).

AFTERNOON

Circuit the trendy **Freihausviertel** (p106)
and enjoy a lunch lovingly made by
elderly folk at the homely **Vollpension**
(p106). Walk to neighbouring
Karlsplatz and admire the baroque
Karlskirche (St Charles's Church;
pictured above; p101), inside and out.

EVENING

Head to the buzzing **Naschmarkt**
(p107), an outdoor market where
restaurants keep the vibe going until
late evening. Finish with cocktails
at Mariahilf's **Miranda Bar** (p109) or
Neubau's **Die Parfümerie** (p125).

A Short Break

MORNING

View the vast art collections of the
imperial family collated over 600 years
at the **Kunsthistorisches Museum Wien**
(p46). Contemporary art aficionados
can opt for **MuseumsQuartier** (MQ)
for **mumok** and Austrian Modernism
in the **Leopold Museum** (p114).

AFTERNOON

Take a walking tour through the trendiest
of **inner districts** (p118), starting in the
bohemian **Neubau** (7th), through the
architecturally stunning **Josefstadt** (8th)
and ending at **Alsergrund** (9th), home
to the **Sigmund Freud Museum** (p122).

EVENING

Head to **Wurstelprater** (pictured above;
p72) amusement park and pick from the
250 attractions and adrenaline thrills.
Grab a bite in the hip **Karmeliterviertel**
(p79) or at **Danube Canal** (p78)
hangouts like **Motto am Fluss** (p64)
and **Strandbar Herrman** (p93).

If You Have More Time

Sample local wine varieties, including Riesling and Grüner Veltliner, at the metropolis-fringing vineyards in the 19th district, or at the 16th's **10er Marie** (p125) – the oldest *Heuriger* (wine tavern) in the city, dating back to 1740. Vienna is the only European capital growing significant amounts of wine within its city limits.

———————————————

Lace up your hiking boots and take an urban ramble. Choose from 14 **Stadtwanderwege** (city walking trails; p75), from neighbourhood parks to the Vienna hills and up the 'mountains' of Kahlenberg and Leopoldsberg.

Rent a motor, pedalo or row boat and cruise the waters of the grassy bathing bank-lined **Alte Donau** (p78) or lounge at the human-made sands of **Copa Beach** (p78) or the bougie **Vienna City Beach Club** (p78) complex on the Neue Donau.

———————————————

Step beyond the pomp of Schönbrunn Palace and into the former imperial hunting ground turned nature reserve **Lainzer Tiergarten** (p136), for a city-view hike or a peek into Empress Elisabeth's park-set summer palace **Hermesvilla** (p136).

———————————————

Lainzer Tiergarten (p136)

IBRIX/SHUTTERSTOCK

A Day Trip

Take a one-hour train from Vienna to Krems or Melk – the gateways to the fortress-topped medieval hamlets and apricot tree-backed, terraced stone-wall vineyards of the **Wachau Valley** (p138) that ribbon beside the Danube River.

Between the two towns, hike the **Wachau World Heritage Trail** (p138), bike a segment of the **Danube Cycle Path** (p138) or take it all in slowly on a scenic cruise or rail ride between cobbled laneway **Krems** (p138) and monumental baroque abbey icon **Melk** (p138).

Along the way, consider stops at pastel-hued **Dürnstein** (p138) and its hillside castle ruins (pictured above), **Domäne Wachau** (p139) for wine tasting, and the idyllic village of **Spitz** (p139).

On a Rainy Day

More than its masterpiece monoliths, Vienna's cache of over 100 museums includes niche and quirky options like the 3rd district **Fälschermuseum** (Museum of Art Fakes; p94) and the world's only **Globenmuseum** (p59) in the historic centre.

Linger for longer In a homely coffee house. Start with a traditional Viennese breakfast (savoury *Semmel* bread roll with butter and jam) and enjoy a lunchtime *Würstchen* (Frankfurter sausage) or cheese-ham toast at the unpolished, old-timer grandmaster **Café Jelinek** (p108).

Tour the interiors of **Ringstrasse landmarks** (p56), including the Rathaus, Opera House, Parliament and the University. Catch a classical concert at the **Musikverein** (pictured above; p61) or basement beats at jazz venue **Porgy & Bess** (p63). 21

Get Prepared

BOOK AHEAD

Three months before
Book accommodation, earlier for the summer and Christmas market seasons, and secure the best-priced opera seats.

One month before
Make reservations at popular restaurants, especially weekend nights, and book tickets for classical concerts and the **Spanish Riding School** (p39).

One week before
Prebook time-slot tickets for high-profile sites like **Belvedere** (p86), **Schönbrunn** (p130), the **Sisi Museum** (p38) and the **Imperial Apartments** (p38).

Manners Matter

When entering smaller and independent stores, it is customary to greet the staff with *Grüss Gott* (hello), and when leaving, either *Auf Wiederschauen* (goodbye) or *Danke* (thank you).

During lunchtime, Austrians wish everyone *Mahlzeit*, a greeting to enjoy the meal before digging in. Every drink will be raised with a *Prost* (cheers) while keeping eye contact – not doing so is considered rude.

Unique Viennese Humour

You may find the Viennese blunt and grumpy at times, especially in customer service. But note that it's part of the local charm and nothing personal. It's a mix of the mellow *Passt scho'* (everything is okay) attitude and the *Wiener Schmäh* humour (think British sarcasm but with more bite). Should you take too long to order, be too demanding or ask an obvious question, you may experience such wit in action.

Things to Know

Closing times Many museums are closed on either Monday or Tuesday. Supermarkets and shops are closed on Sunday. In July and August, some drinking and dining locales close for the summer break.

Carry cash While Visa and MasterCard are more widely accepted than American Express and Diners Club, many establishments still don't accept cards at all. Establishments where you can only pay with *Bargeld* (cash) usually display such terms, but it pays to ask before you order.

Vienna is a safe city in general Visitors should have no trouble walking around at night; however, some areas are best avoided, or may feel unnerving for some. Prater and Praterstern can get dodgy after dark; the area north of Westbahnhof, from Felberstrasse to the Gürtel's cluster of red-light clubs, can be seedy.

TIPPING

Unless service is terrible, it's considered rude not to tip in Vienna.

10%

Restaurants
at least 10%

10%

Bars and cafes
10% or round up
to the nearest
euro or two

€2/10

Hotel staff
porters/
concierge
for excellent
service

€1

**Cloakroom
attendants**

DAILY BUDGET

BUDGET: Less than €100

- Dorm bed in a hostel with breakfast: **€45**
- Light bites, *Würstelstand* snacks and lunchtime specials: **€5–15**
- Daily transport ticket: **€10.20**
- Standing ticket at the opera: **€18**

MIDRANGE: €100–200

- Double room in a trendy hotel: **€90–120**
- Two-course dinner with a glass of wine: **€35**
- High-profile museum admission: **€21**
- Guided group walking tour: **€35**

TOP END: More than €200

- Double room in an upmarket hotel: **from €160**
- Upscale restaurant dinner with wine: **from €100**
- Premium Musikverein tickets: **€139**
- Spanish Riding School performance tickets: **from €60**

Currency
Euro (€)

Language
German

Time zone
Central European
Time (UTC/GMT
plus one hour).

TIP

The **Vienna City Card** *(viennacitycard.at)* provides unlimited travel on public transport and discounts across hundreds of selected museums, guided tours, coffee houses, restaurants and shops. Purchase online, or at Tourist Info Wien at the airport or on Albertinaplatz.

23

📅 When to Go

Vienna is a year-round cultural hub where museums, music stages and coffee houses hum regardless of the weather and the city's open-air festivities change with the seasons.

Spring (March to May) marks the start of the tourism season. The city's *Schanigarten* (streetside and restaurant gardens) bloom and life is all about the great outdoors, despite inconsistent weather. In summer (June to August) warmer temperatures bring a programme of street, square and park festivals, and days spent riverside boating and bathing. Temperatures fall in autumn (September and October), and the city's green blanket turns golden. Vienna peaks in winter (November to February) when Christmas markets open, ice rinks are set up and the city waltzes to Ball Season.

Traditional Events

November & December: Vienna enchants during Advent with wonder-filled, hut-lined **Wiener Christkindlmärkte**.

November–February: The city waltzes on the streets during **New Year** celebrations and at more than 400 prestigious soirees during **Ball Season**.

March: Easter Markets open until Easter Sunday, laden with crafts, food and drink.

June: Head lawn-side for the free **Summer Night Concert** (p135) of the Wiener Philharmoniker (Vienna Philharmonic) at Schönbrunn Palace.

September: Locals hike between vineyards during the two-day *wein* celebration, **Wiener Weinwandertag** (Vienna Wine Hiking Day).

October: Pack in as many of the city's museums from 6pm until 1am, with a single ticket during the **Long Night of the Museums**.

Vienna Weather

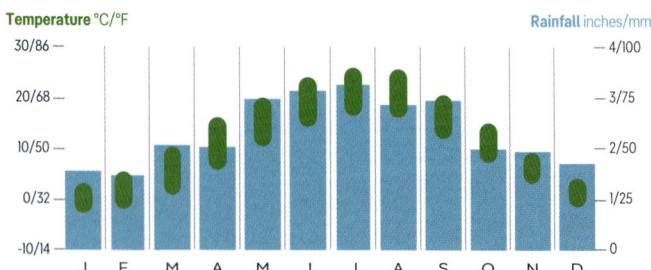

Temperature °C/°F — Rainfall inches/mm

OLD TOWN TOURIST/SHUTTERSTOCK

Film Festival Rathausplatz

Contemporary & Expressive

May: **Wiener Festwochen** (Vienna Festival Week) kicks off spring with a mega programme of performance arts. The Stadtpark crams in a regional gastronomic showcase during the **Genuss Festival**.

June: The Donauinsel (Danube Island) is a weekend party during Europe's biggest free open-air music festival, **Donauinselfest**. The **Regenbogen Parade** (Rainbow Parade; p146) Pride event circles the city and ends at a festive-bound Rathausplatz.

July: The City Hall square turns into an open-air cinema during the two-month-long **Film Festival Rathausplatz** with music films

from concert and opera greats, plus food stalls. **Popfest** (p103), the four-day experimental music festival with Austrian acts, has its main stage at Karlsplatz.

August: Up-and-coming artists top the stages set up along the bar-lined *Gürtel* (belt) road during the **Gürtel Night Walk** on the last weekend of the month. The annual **Calle Libre Festival** invites artists to paint murals and the public to tour urban artwork displays.

September: Marvel at circus acts, acrobatics, fire shows, dance and more during the three-day performance art **Buskers Festival** at Karlsplatz.

--- **BOOK YOUR STAY** ---

Snag better-priced rooms during the shoulder seasons (April to May and September to November) when crowds ease and the weather is moderate; prices can drop even more during Vienna's coldest and quietest months (January to March). Rates peak during the summer and Christmas market seasons.

✈ Getting There

Most visitors arrive in the city via Vienna International Airport (Schwechat), located 18km southeast of the historical centre, although it's also easily reached by intercity train and international bus from Europe.

From the Airport to the City Centre

By Train

The nonstop **City Airport Train** (*CAT; cityairporttrain.com; single/return €14.90/24.90*) leaves the airport every 30 minutes for Wien-Mitte Landstrasse station from 6.07am to 11.37pm daily. The journey takes 16 minutes.

S7 suburban trains (*S-Bahn; €4.40*) run the same route to Wien-Mitte Landstrasse and depart every 30 minutes from 05.19am to 00.19am. The journey takes 25 minutes.

High-speed ÖBB RJ and RJX trains (*oebb.at; €4.60*) depart for Hauptbahnhof station every 30 minutes from 6.33am to 00.02am. The journey takes 15 minutes.

By Bus

Vienna Airport Lines (*vienna airportlines.at; single/return €11/20*) runs three bus services; two connect the airport to the centre with departures every 30 minutes. Line 1 to Hauptbahnhof (25 minutes) and Westbahnhof (45 minutes) runs from 4.30am to 3.30am. Line 2 to Morzinplatz/Schwedenplatz (22 minutes) runs from 4.10am to 11.45pm.

By Taxi

A metered taxi from the airport can cost €50 or more. The yellow **Taxi 40100** (*taxi40100.at*) has a fixed rate of €42; the transfer desk is in the Terminal 3 arrivals hall. A trip using a rideshare app costs between €30 and €40.

Other Points of Entry

Vienna Central Train Station

Wien Hauptbahnhof, Vienna's main station, is the hub for international services and ÖBB Railjet (RJ) and NightJet (NJ). Located 3km south of the historic centre, you can get into the city via the U1 metro line Südtiroler Platz station, which stops at Karlsplatz, Stephansplatz and Prater; trams D towards the Ringstrasse, O to Landstrasse and Praterstern; and bus 13A, which loops through the Vorstädte (inner districts) 5th (Margareten), 6th (Mariahilf), 7th (Neubau) and 8th (Josefstadt) between the Ringstrasse and the Gürtel.

Vienna Central Bus Station (VIB)

The VIB (the main international bus terminal) is in Erdberg, opposite the U3 metro line Erdberg stop, serving Flixbus routes – though some buses also use Wien Hauptbahnhof and Westbahnhof.

Getting Around

Vienna's spiral of 23 districts are well connected by an efficient public transportation system. The historic centre and inner districts are easy to explore on foot, including museum complexes, modern neighbourhoods with landmarks and low-key nightlife. Schloss Schönbrunn is a little further out but can easily be reached by bus, tram and metro from the centre.

Walking

Compact central Vienna is perfect for strolling between sites, from grand palaces to pretty set-stone streets. You can walk from the Danube Canal to the Hofburg in 18 minutes, Rathaus to Stadtpark in 30, and around the architectural belt Ringstrasse (ring road) in one hour; from there you can easily navigate into the inner districts.

Metro

Vienna's underground rail (U-Bahn) is the fastest and most efficient way of getting around. Five lines are currently in operation: U1 to U4 and the U6, with a sixth line (U5) due for completion in 2026. All lines run from 5am to midnight and 24 hours on Friday and Saturday. Maps are easy to read, platforms have timetable information and announcements are also in English. All stations have wheelchair access.

Tram

Vienna's trams (*Bim*; denoted by number or letter; pictured above) are a slower but visually rewarding journey, especially on the Ringstrasse and the approach to

FROM LEFT: PORNPRASIT PANADA/SHUTTERSTOCK, 4KCLIPS/SHUTTERSTOCK

─── **ESSENTIAL APP** ───
Download the **WienMobil app** for ticket purchase, departure times and route planning.

Schönbrunn. They typically run from around 5am to midnight.

Bus

While trickier to navigate than the metro, buses are reliable and punctual, linking all corners of the city. Most run from 5am to midnight; services can be sporadic or non-existent on weekends. Night buses (marked with an 'N') run from 12.30am to 5am, every 30 minutes, with many departing from points on the Ring.

Bike

WienMobil Rad (wienerlinien.at/ wienmobil/rad), Vienna's low-cost public bike-rental service, has 185 pick-up/drop-off stations across all districts; the city has over 1600km of cycle paths. Rides are charged in 30-minute increments (at €0.75) with a 24-hour cap of €19.

Taxis

Taxis, while relatively cheap by western standards, are a pricey way to get around. City journeys are metered. Daytime tariffs (6am–11pm) have a minimum charge of €3.80 and a per kilometre fee up to €0.95; night tariffs (11pm–6am) charge a slightly higher rate; and phone reservations have a €2 surcharge. Check if it's a cash or card payment before hopping in.

Public Transport Essentials

Integrated System

Flat fare single journey tickets are valid for Wiener Linien services (U-Bahn, trams and buses) in the core zone of Vienna; there are no peak hour charges or set-time tariffs.

Single tickets are good for one journey, including line and transport changes, and are valid for up to 80 minutes. Services are frequent and you'll rarely be waiting more than 10 minutes.

Where to Buy Tickets

Tickets can be purchased at main station ticket offices and at machines in U-Bahn station entrances and on the trams (but not directly from bus drivers). Tabak Trafik (Tabakladen; tobacco kiosks) also sell them.

There are no ticket barriers or tap-on/tap-off cards. Paper tickets must be validated before (on the U-Bahn) or immediately upon boarding (buses and trams). If you purchase a ticket from a machine there is the option to 'Validate Now'. Sporadic checks take place on board, but more often at the platform exits.

Digital tickets are available via the WienMobil app (and cost around 5% less), where you will be asked to choose a start station and add the passenger's name. A validated ticket will be displayed.

Discounted Ticket Passes

Children up to the age of six travel free; children under 15 years can travel for half price *(€1.60; single fare)*.

Discounts for visitors include the **QueerCityPass** *(queercitypass. com; 24hr ticket €15.90)*, which includes reduced entry and deals at attractions and establishments alongside unlimited travel, much like the **Vienna City Card** *(vienna citycard.at; 24hr ticket €17)*.

Fare Evasion

Getting caught without a valid ticket results in a €105 (immediate cash payment) fine.

TRAVEL COSTS

Bike rental
per 30 minutes
€0.75

Single journey fare
€3.20

24-hour transport ticket
€10.20

VALIDATE YOUR TICKET

Stamp paper tickets at the blue machines in underground stations and on buses and trams.

TICKETS

Ticket	Fee	Info
Single journey	€3.20	One journey within 80 minutes (including changes)
24-hour ticket	€10.20	Valid from the specified start date and time
Weekly ticket	€28.90	Valid for seven consecutive days from the specified start date

TICKET ZONES

Kernzone
The 'core zone' covers the city of Vienna and is where all major sights are located.

Zone 2
Where Vienna International Airport is located; a ticket extension is required.

A Few Surprises

Scratch Vienna's gleaming imperial surface and find wartime relics, bold Modernist architecture and a creative embrace of unusual subjects.

'Proletariat Palaces'

The aftermath of the monarchy's collapse and postwar impoverishment fuelled the ruling Social Democratic Workers' Party's reforms centred around urban communal living. The period from 1919 to 1934, known as 'Red Vienna', saw the construction of around 400 *Gemeindebauten* – mega-apartment estates with all-encompassing social infrastructure including clinics, kindergartens, green space and amenities. These recognisable buildings dot almost every district, seamlessly standing alongside their ornamental 19th-century neighbours; it's a legacy still in operation, with around one in four Viennese citizens living in social housing. The largest of these red landmarks is the 1930-built Karl-Marx-Hof in the 19th district. It's the longest continuous residential building in the world, stretching over 1100 metres through Heiligenstadt.

Towering Wartime Shelters

Today's picturesque metropolis is pierced by grey, brutalist relics of WWII: six concrete **Flaktürme** (flak towers; p78), above-ground air-raid-defence bunkers from the early 1940s that Hitler ordered to be built to protect the city from Allied airstrikes. Constructed in pairs, two punctuate the baroque Augarten (2nd district), and another pair rises above the urban Arenbergpark (3rd district). The remaining were repurposed: Esterházy Park's tower (6th district) is now the city's aquarium **Haus des Meeres** and rooftop 360° OCEAN SKY bar and restaurant, and the other is part of the Stiftskaserne military barracks (7th district).

A Deathly Fascination

The Viennese morbid sense of humour in regard to death is showcased at the **Zentralfriedhof** (Central Cemetery) **Funeral Museum**,

---

OFFBEAT VIENNA

Austria's capital, proud of its cleanliness, invites you on a surprising, subterranean expedition of its waste-water system on the **Sewer Tour** (p103).

See historical layers in modern spaces, like fragments of Vienna's medieval city walls in the U3 metro station, at the **Stubentor** (p58).

Hidden within Stephansplatz metro, stand within the foundations of the 800-year-old chapel, **Virgilka-pelle** (p58), which lies beneath Stephansdom.

Take a look at the uniquely preserved corpses in the lesser-visited noble burial vault at the **Michael-erkirche** (p42).

Kirche am Steinhof

a compact walk through the city's centuries-long unique relationship with mortality, burial traditions and funeral customs. Browse funerary attire, hearse design and coffin inventions, including a seated casket, recyclable coffins and a fitted bell mechanism in case of premature burial. The gift shop stocks merch adorned with witty slogans and graveyard-inspired Lego sets. The *Würstelstand* at the cemetery's entrance is aptly named 'eh scho wuascht' – Viennese slang for 'it doesn't matter anymore'.

20th-Century Art Heirlooms

Take an Art Deco dip in the Amalienbad (10th district) and Jörgerbad (17th district) indoor pool heirlooms of 1920s Vienna, or spend an Art Nouveau penny at the Adolf Loos–designed public toilets on the opulent Graben shopping street.

Otto Wagner

The gilded-domed **Kirche am Steinhof** at the foot of the Gallitzinberg (14th district) bears the hallmarks of Otto Wagner's Modernist visions, with a copper-detailed and marble-clad exterior and a functional, attention-to-detail interior. Europe's first modern church was crafted to meet the needs of the patients of the psychiatric hospital below; on the path up, visitors unknowingly walk past the 1907 clinical complex Wagner conceptualised. The 60 Art Nouveau pavilions underwent numerous infirmary iterations over time. Today the area designated as the **Otto Wagner Areal** (*owa-wien.at*) is helping to preserve a catalogue of listed buildings that form part of Vienna's architectural heritage, reimagined through a cultural programme of events and exhibitions.

Explore Vienna

View from Stephansdom's North Tower (p44)
ROMAS_PHOTO/SHUTTERSTOCK

See p64
for eating,
drinking and
shopping
listings

Explore
Historic Centre: Innere Stadt

The oldest of the 23 *Bezirke,* Vienna's 1st district is its cobbled-street, pastel-hue-tinged, boulevard-ringed historical heart. It's a layering of centuries compacted in a 3-sq-km open-air museum: Roman ruins reveal the foundations of the military encampment of Vindobona; the noble thread of the Middle Ages runs through the Gothic thoroughfares; the palatial Hofburg complex and art arsenals of the Habsburg Empire still stand; horse-drawn carriages rumble along timeless streets; and the coffee house culture continues. Soaring from its core is the 136m Gothic masterpiece and city symbol, Stephansdom, nexus of a heritage so significant that UNESCO enshrined the Innere Stadt as a World Heritage Site.

Getting Around

 Walk

The historic core is easily navigated on foot. Book a tour via the *Fiaker* horse-drawn carriage at Stephansplatz and Michaelerplatz.

U-Bahn (Metro)

Herrengasse (U3) is located next to the Hofburg; Stephansplatz (U1, U3) directly outside the Cathedral; and Stubentor (U3) opposite the Stadtpark. MuseumsQuartier (U2) is convenient for the museums on Maria-Theresien-Platz and Karlsplatz (U1, U2, U4) for the Wiener Staatsoper.

 Tram

Trams 1 and 2 circuit the Ringstrasse; D and 71 cover its western loop.

Pestsäule (Plague Column) on the Graben (p55)

THE BEST

HISTORICAL MONUMENT
Hofburg (p38)

IMPERIAL MUSEUM
Kaiserappartements and Sisi Museum (p38)

VIEWPOINT
Stephansdom (p44)

ART GALLERY
Kunsthistorisches Museum (p46)

CULTURAL EXPERIENCE
Vienna Coffee House Culture (p65)

A

B

C

D

Liebiggasse

Grillparzerstr.

1

Ebendorferstr.

Universität Wien

Melker Bastei

Schottengasse

Helferstorferstr.

Freyung

Wipplingerstr.

32

50

Reichsratsstr.

Rathausstr.

Rathausplatz

Felderstr.

Teinfaltstr.

20
Beethoven Pasqualatihaus

Tiefer Graben

Färbergasse

Wallnerstr.

41

Rathauspark

Löwelstr.

66

Am Hof

Bognergasse

Naglergasse

Herrengasse

35

Lichtenfelsgasse

22
Wiener Christkindlmarkt am Rathausplatz

Rathausplatz/ Burgtheater

Bankgasse

INNERE STADT 1

Globenmuseum

30

65

Rathauspark

Minoritenplatz
10

61

63
36

Stadiongasse

Stadiongasse/ Parlament

Ballhausplatz

Herrengasse

Doblhoffgasse

Österreichisches Parlament

Löwelstr.

Volksgarten

Michaelerplatz

Time Travel Vienna
9

Kaiserappartements

3

Dr Karl- Renner-Ring

Schmerlingplatz

Schmerlingplatz

Sisi Museum
In der Burg

1
Michaelerplatz Roman Ruins

Hofburg

Kaiserliche Schatzkammer

Justizpalast
6

Ring/Volkstheater

Heldenplatz

16
Vienna Hofburg Orchestra

Josefsplatz

Burgring (Ringstrasse)

Bellariastr.

4

Museumsplatz

Volksgartenstr.

Naturhistorisches Museum

Papyrusmuseum

Ephesos Museum
11

Weltmuseum

Augustinerstr.

Volkstheater

Maria- Theresien- Platz

Neue Burg

Burggarten

Goethegasse

Volkstheater

NEUBAU

Breite Gasse

Museumsplatz

Burgring

Babenbergerstr.

Kunsthistorisches Museum

Opernring (Ringstrasse)

5

Hanuschgasse

For more see

Top Experiences ⭐ p38
Experiences ✳️ p58
Eating 🍴 p64
Drinking 🍷 p65
Shopping 🛍️ p66

Museumsquartier

Elisabethstr.

Schillerplatz

Nibelungengasse

Operngasse

Rahngasse

Getreidemarkt

6

N
0   400 m
0   0.2 miles

Secession
23

Friedrichstr.

Girardipark

Karlsplatz

A

B

C

D

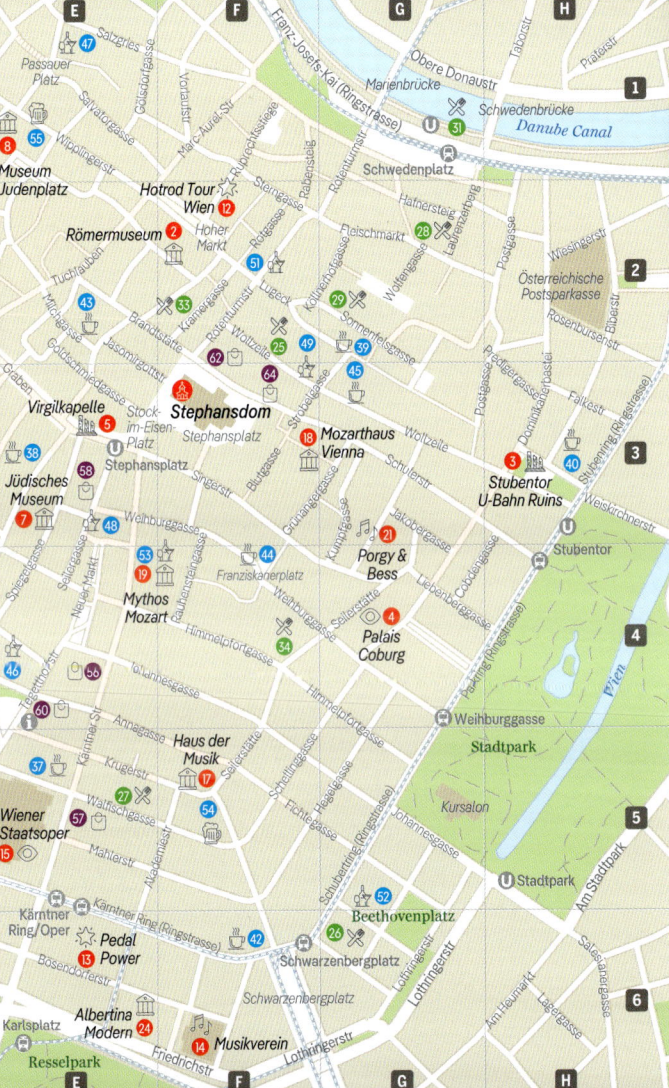

E **F** **G** **H**

Obere Donaustr

Franz-Josefs-Kai (Ringstrasse)

Marienbrücke

1

Schwedenbrücke

Danube Canal

31

Schwedenplatz

Salzgries

47

Passauer
Platz

Wippingerstr

8 **55**

Museum
Judenplatz

Hotrod Tour
Wien **12**

Römermuseum **2**

Hoher
Markt

Fleischmarkt

28

2

Österreichische
Postsparkasse

51

43 **33**

29

62 **64**

25 **49** **39**

45

Virgilkapelle

Stock-
im-Eisen-
Platz

5

Stephansdom

18 Mozarthaus
Vienna

Stephansplatz

Wollzeile

3 **40** **3**

Stubentor
U-Bahn Ruins

38

Jüdisches
Museum

58

Stephansplatz

Schulerstr

Stubentor

7

48

Weihburggasse

53

19

44

21

Porgy &
Bess

Mythos
Mozart

Franziskanerplatz

4

Palais
Coburg

34

46

56

4

Wien

Weihburggasse

Stadtpark

60

Haus der
Musik

37

Krugerstr

17

Kursalon

27

54

Wiener
Staatsoper

57

5

15

Stadtpark

Kärntner
Ring/Oper

Pedal
Power

42

52

Beethovenplatz

13

26

Schwarzenbergplatz

6

Schwarzenbergplatz

Albertina
Modern

24

14 Musikverein

Karlsplatz

Resselpark

Lothringerstr

E **F** **G** **H**

37

EXPLORE

HISTORIC CENTRE: INNERE STADT

Hofburg

Nothing epitomises the extravagant reign of the Habsburgs more than the humongous 240,000-sq-metre Hofburg. The sovereign home and seven-century-long power base of the imperial family up until 1918 packs a staggering collection of cultural artefacts, art masterpieces and classical equestrianism into its 18 wings and 19 courtyards.

MAP P36 **C3**

PLANNING TIP

The complex is open 24 hours, but the imperial museum hours vary; some open from 9.30am to 5.30pm, others from 10am to 6pm. Last admission is typically one hour before closing.

Scan this QR code for info on discounted entry to this multi-museum complex with the Vienna City Card.

Imperial Heritage in the Alte Burg Museums

Start in the Alte Burg's (Old Castle) gilded Imperial Chancellery Wing and Amalia Residence at the **Sisi Museum** and **Kaiserappartements** (*Imperial Apartments; sisimuseum-hofburg.at; adult/child €20/12*). You'll enter via the marbled Emperor's Staircase before roaming through 17 resplendent rooms of court life, accompanied by a 75-minute audio guide. The misunderstood life and final days of Empress Elisabeth are sensitively covered; 300 personal items – from childhood trinkets to beauty items, gloves and replica gowns – are on display, as is her death mask, made after her assassination in Geneva in 1898. Move on to the dazzling belt of living spaces, including bedrooms and bathrooms, studies and saloons, preserved with their chandeliered ceilings, decked walls, regal red silk upholstery and royal gold embellishments.

Within the wings of the Schweizerhof (Swiss Courtyard), the **Kaiserliche Schatzkammer Wien** (*Imperial Treasury Vienna; kaiserliche-schatzkammer.at; adult/child €18/free*) presents a millennium of crown jewel majesty with its Holy Roman and Habsburg Empire heirlooms. Highlights of imperial regalia include the jewelled Crown and Holy Lance of Emperor Rudolf II (Room 2); the precious stone and pearl-adorned Imperial Crown of the Holy Roman Empire of the

German Nation (Room 11); and the distinguished insignia of the Order of the Golden Fleece (Room 15). The wood-panelled **Sacred Treasury** holds rare religious relics, including a cross nail from Christ's crucifixion, the divinely imprinted face of Jesus on the Veil of Veronica and a piece of cloth from the Last Supper.

The classical skills of horse-riding and equestrianship have been practised at the **Spanische Hofreitschule** (*Spanish Riding School; srs.at; adult/children from €26/reduced admission*) with white Lipizzaner stallions since 1565. This unique preservation of equestrianism only exists here, and is on both the Intangible Cultural Heritage and Intangible Heritage of Humanity UNESCO lists. Every rider is responsible for the daily training of their small group of horses to perfect the graceful skills proudly demonstrated in the famed musical performances in the baroque **Winter Riding School** arena. Performances

QUICK BREAK
Stop for a classic Viennese sausage at the long-running **Bitzinger Würstelstand am Albertinaplatz**. The green rabbit sculpture on top is a nod to Dürer's precious work inside the Albertina.

VIENNA BOYS' CHOIR
The **Vienna Boys' Choir** *(wsk.at; from €14)* performs during Holy Mass in the Burgkapelle at 9:15am Sundays between September and June. Book your ticket ahead of time.

are held only on weekends; training sessions on weekday mornings. Guided tours of the Spanish Riding School run daily; architecture tours on Saturday afternoons.

Curated Culture in the Neue Burg Museums

The arc wing of the **Neue Burg** (New Castle) and the forecourt **Heldenplatz** (Heroes Sq) mark the grand expansion of the Hofburg in the late 19th century. An imperial guesthouse was planned for the Corps de Logis wing, but it has instead been home to one of the world's most important ethnographic collections since 1928 – the personal souvenirs amassed by the three Habsburg Archdukes, Ferdinand Max, Crown Prince Rudolf and Franz Ferdinand, during their expeditions throughout the 1800s.

SYLVAIN SONNET/GETTY IMAGES

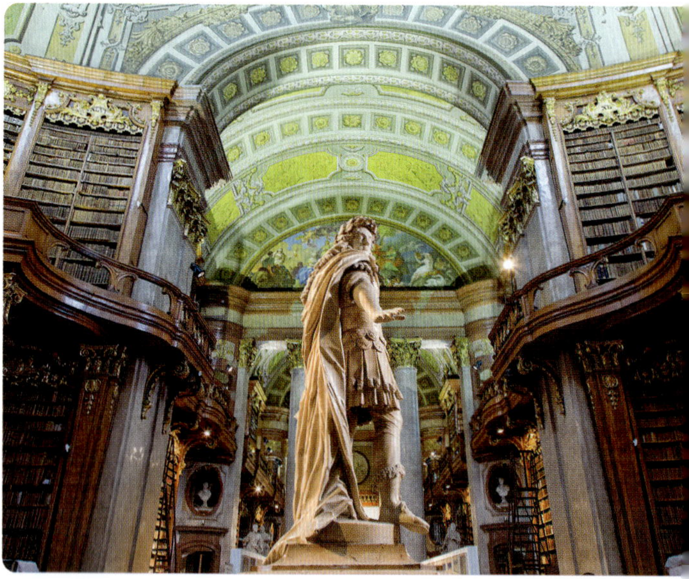

Following his 10-month world voyage in 1892, Franz Ferdinand envisioned what is now the **Weltmuseum** (*World Museum; weltmuseumwien.at; adult/child €16/free*). Across 14 halls on the middle floor is a permanent exhibit of a mind-blowing 250,000 anthropological objects from outside Europe, accompanied by objects, drawings, photographs and scientific notes from other explorers, including British seafarer James Cook and German naturalist Otto Finch. Notably, an exhibit examines the modern-day conversation about the cause and consequence of Europe's colonial expansion and the plundered, given or exchanged context of acquiring archaeological and cultural relics.

The neighbouring **Ephesos Museum** (*khm.at/en/exhibitions/ephesos-museum; included in House of Austrian History ticket*) is a compilation of the work of Austrian archaeologists who have been excavating the ancient Greek city of Ephesus since 1895. Important statues and friezes from the site, now located in Turkey, were relocated to Vienna; its prized masterpieces include the cherished carved-stone panel reliefs of the Parthian Monument and the Amazon relief from the Temple of Artemis, one of the original Seven Wonders of the World.

Those looking for a detailed timeline and debate on the past 100 years of political events in Austrian history can untangle it all in 57 interactive stations in the thought-provoking **Haus der Geschichte Österreich** (*House of Austrian History; hdgoe.at; adult/child €10/free*) covering the move from monarchy to republic, the annexation of Austria by the Third Reich before WWII, and Austria's place in the European Union.

Baroque Prunksaal

So grand is the nearly 80m-long court library of Habsburg emperor Karl VI that it is stationed in its own dedicated wing. The 18th-century baroque

ORIGINAL FEATURES
Extravagant expansions ravaged the foundational four-towered medieval castle of 1246, though the Hofburg's oldest segment, **Schweizerhof** (Swiss Wing), retains part of the medieval moat. When entering the Renaissance **Schweizertor** (Swiss Gate), added around 1550 during the first upgrades, sections of the incorporated drawbridge ball chains are visible. Some 15th-century Gothic elements of the **Burgkapelle** have also been preserved.

41

SEE THE STALLIONS

You might be lucky to glimpse the Lipizzaner stallions resting in the **Stallburg** (Stable Palace) on Reitschulgasse. During training hours (7am-12.55pm), they cross the street to the Winter Riding School approximately every 30 minutes. The most majestic setting for a sighting is in the Burggarten, between 8.30am and 10am from spring to autumn. Mondays are their day off.

Prunksaal der Österreichischen National-bibliothek (*State Hall of the Austrian National Library; onb.ac.at/museen/prunksaal; adult/child €11/free;* pictured p40), built to elaborate royal taste, is one of the most important libraries in the world. Marble-columned archways open to circular rooms with dark-walnut-wood shelves featuring gilded motifs and magnificent frescoes on the domed ceiling. A statue of the emperor stands in the centre, surrounded by 200,000 leather-bound books, the earliest dating to 1501.

Michaelerplatz & Around

Members of the Habsburg family were not entombed in one place; their body parts were split in three and spread across the city.

The **Herzgruft** (heart burial vault) is in the Loreto Chapel of the 14th-century gothic **Augustinerkirche** (*Augustinian Church; guided tours only after High Mass on Sun; €10);* the intestines in Stephansdom's **Ducal Crypt**; and the rest of the body in the imperial crypt, **Kapuzinergruft** (*Capuchin's Crypt; kapuzinergruft.com; adult/child €13/7),* where 150 Habsburg family members, including Maria Theresia, Empress Elizabeth and Franz Joseph I, have been laid to rest. English tours take place Monday, Wednesday and Saturday.

Not for the faint-hearted, the baroque royal parish of **Michaelerkirche** (*St Michael's Church; michaelerkirche.at; adult/child €8/4, private tours in English up to six people €48)* on Michaelerplatz is a mesh of catacombs filled with the bones of over 4000 people buried here from 1631 to 1784, and the cold rooms of noble crypts that have partially preserved the now mummified bodies. Guided tours are currently only in German.

With a repository of more than one million drawings and prints, the **Albertina** (p63; *albertina.at; adult/child €19.90/free)* houses one of the world's largest collections of graphic art. The permanent Batliner Collection is a showcase of Modernist

GREGOR LECHNER

pieces, featuring works by master sketchers like Monet and Picasso. Its most famous is the 1502 watercolour *Young Hare* by Albrecht Dürer. To resume the imperial gazing, visit the 20 restored luxurious Habsburg State Rooms of this former royal palace (included in admission).

The Imperial Gardens

The **Volksgarten** (public garden), the first built by the Habsburgs for the people, remains a splendid stroll with its Greek Theseus Temple and 3000 fragrant rose bushes. It's not uncommon to see locals lounging on the adjacent **Burggarten** (Palace Garden) lawn. Emperor Franz Joseph's verdant enclosure opened to the public in 1919, and his *Jugendstil* glasshouse jungle turned classy cafe-bar **Palmenhaus** (Palm House; *palmenhaus.at;* pictured above) is shared with the tropical **Schmetterlinghaus** (Butterfly House), with hundreds of colourful flutterers.

GETTING AROUND
Use **St Michael's Gate** on Michaelerplatz to enter the Alte Burg complex; the **Outer Gate** for the Neue Burg; the **Swiss Gate** for the Imperial Treasury; and **Josefsplatz** for the Prunksaal.

43

⭐ **TOP EXPERIENCE**

Stephansdom

No other landmark symbolises the city more than the Gothic masterpiece that is the Stephansdom (St Stephen's Cathedral), rising from the centre of the Innere Stadt. Marvel as its filigree nave, reach its soaring heights in towers with panoramic views and take a sombre tour through its *Katakomben* (catacombs).

MAP P36 **F3**

PLANNING TIP

If you plan to visit all cathedral sites, consider the all-inclusive ticket *(adult/child €25/7)*. It includes entry to the ecclesiastical art and antiquities of the Treasury of the Teutonic Order.

Scan this QR code for opening hours, and concert and events listings.

Stephansdom Inside & Out

A church has stood on this site since the early 12th century, with original Romanesque elements still visible today in the **Riesentor** (Giant's Gate) and **Heidentürme** (Heathen Towers) at the cathedral's entrance and above it. Stephansdom's three-century-long Gothic glow-up peaked with its 136.4m South Tower in 1433 and was cut short in its half-finished 68.3m-high domed North Tower by 1578. A chevron mosaic of 230,000 glazed roof tiles crests in between, stamped with the imperial double-headed eagle.

It's free to venture into the vaulted, prismatic glass site, though it is a bit of a scrum. Paid entry allows for a closer look at the 16th-century Gothic sandstone masterwork on the **Pilgramkanzel** (Pilgrim pulpit) and the commanding baroque black marble **High Altar**, which consecrated the holy space some 100 years later.

Admission *(incl digital audio guide adult/child €6/2)* is on the left side aisle facing the altar; payments are in cash only. Thirty-minute guided tours *(adult/child €7/3)* give detailed insight into the interior features; English tours take place at 10.30am Monday to Friday. For worshippers only, the central nave is free to enter during Mass.

Towering High

An elevator takes you to the Stephansplatz-looming **North Tower** *(adult/child €7/3)* platform for

MISTERVLAD/SHUTTERSTOCK

Austria's largest bell, the 21-tonne Pummerin, installed here in 1957. It only rings in the New Year.

For sweeping historic centre city views from the **South Tower** *(adult/child €6.50/2.50)* you must climb 343 precarious, winding steps to access the peering *Türmerstube* (tower room). Entrance is outside the cathedral at Stephansplatz 1.

Beneath the Cathedral

The area around the cathedral was originally a graveyard, but by 1732 it had closed, moving burials underground. In the depths of the **Katakomben** *(adult/child €7/3)* wander from the noble burial chambers and imperial Ducal Crypt displaying the urns of the internal organs of the Habsburgs into the sombre, bone-stacked ossuary caverns – the resting place for the more than 10,000 people who perished during the Great Plague of 1679.

QUICK BREAK
Feast on *Frittatensuppe* (sliced pancakes in beef broth), *Wiener Schnitzel, Gulasch* and more at **Gasthaus Reinthaler**, one of the historic district's last remaining authentic *Beisl* (taverns) from 1977.

★ TOP EXPERIENCE

Kunsthistorisches Museum

The Kunsthistorisches Museum Wien is the jewel in the crown of the city's art assemblage – a magnificent Habsburg treasure house that has been displaying master works and curiosities from ancient Egypt, Rome and Greece and the Renaissance and baroque periods to the public since 1891.

MAP P36 **B5**

PLANNING TIP
It's best to tackle the museum one floor at a time. Following the chronological order of exhibits, start on the ground floor and work your way up.

Scan this QR code to prebook admission tickets and bypass long queues.

Egyptian & Near Eastern Collection

From the Cupola Hall entrance, ascend the stairs immediately to the right for a 5000-year dynastic dive into the Egyptian and Near Eastern Collection (Level 0.5), covering the Predynastic Period to the Christian Era. Enter the first hall with paintings created by Ernst Weidenbach in 1873, re-creating scenes from the Beni Hasan tomb of Chnumhotep II.

Take a left to Room II and stand within the ❶ **Offering Chapel of Ka-ni-nisut** – the re-created funerary cult of the early 5th-century Dynastic official, discovered in Giza in 1913. Continue to Room V for the symbolic statuette of the ❷ **Blue Hippopotamus** and muse the mysteries behind the displays of Egyptian sarcophagi and canopic jars (organ urns), burial offerings and stone-carved reliefs.

Greek & Roman Antiquities

Skip millennia to Room X and enter the Collection of Greek and Roman Antiquities. Admire the carved marble masterwork of the ❸ **Amazon Sarcophagus** relief and the mythological scene-setting floor **Mosaic of Theseus** in Room XI and the captivating gem-carved ❹ **Gemma Augustea Cameo** in Room XVI, glorifying the reign of Emperor Augustus.

ANDREI RYBACHUK/SHUTTERSTOCK

Kunstkammer Wien

The adjacent wing is devoted to the *Kunstkammer Wien* (cabinet of art and curiosities) – a window into the royal fashion of collecting all that was peculiar and precious, such as the ivory-carved **⑤ Apollo and Daphne statuette** in Room XX, clockmaker Hans Schlottheim's magnificently mechanised **⑥ Automaton in the form of a ship** in XXVII and Benvenuto Cellini's golden **⑦ Saliera tableware** in Room XXIX.

Finding Klimt

Ascend the grand marble staircase to the First Floor, where you'll pass Antonio Canova's marble **⑧ Theseus Slaying the Centaur** statue before entering the colossal compilation of Renaissance and baroque paintings in the Gemäldegalerie (Picture Gallery).

Look out for **⑨ The Spandrels** wall murals above the arches and between the columns of the

QUICK BREAK
Refuel with a house roast *Wiener Melange* coffee and a very Viennese snack, *Käse-Schinken* toast (cheese and ham toast), at the bohemian coffee-house institution, **Café Hawelka** (p65).

Kunsthistorisches Museum

Ground Floor

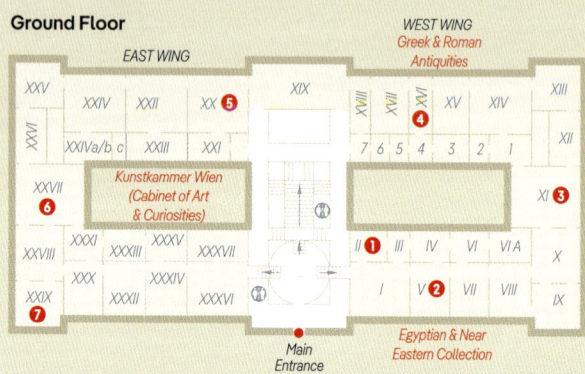

First Floor: Gemäldegalerie (Picture Gallery)

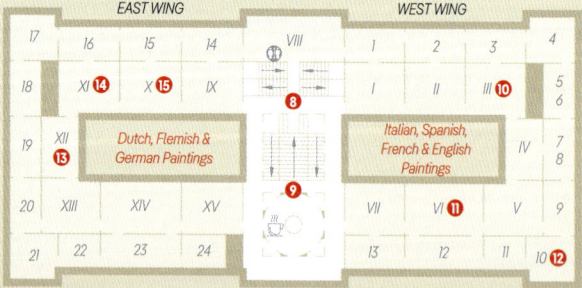

Main Staircase. Gustav Klimt's signature gold-leaf figures encapsulate the museum's collections. The centre figures represent ancient Egypt and ancient Greece. Above the left arch, the Roman and Venetian Quattrocento, and from the right, Early Italian Painting.

Italian, Spanish & French Paintings

The ollection of old masters is the museum's most impressive cache. Turn right into the halls for Italian, Spanish and French painting masterpieces, including Raphael's bucolic ❿ **Madonna of the Meadow** in Room III, Caravaggio's devoted ⓫ **Madonna of the Rosary** in Room VI and Velázquez' defining portrait ⓬ **Infanta Margarita in a Blue Dress** in Room 10.

Dutch, Flemish & German Paintings

Continue past the Lounge to the opposite wing for the Dutch, Flemish and German painting rooms. Take in Vermeer's muse in ⓭ **The Art of Painting** in Room XII en route to Dürer's altarpiece ⓮ **Adoration of the Trinity** in Room XI, and end on a high with Pieter Bruegel the Elder's entrancing ⓯ **The Tower of Babel** in Room X.

Münzkabinett

On the Second Floor, step into one of the largest coin collections in the world in the Münzkabinett. The **Imperial Coin Collection** money cabinet spans three millennia across three halls. The first displays medals of honour from those first used in Italy around 1400 to European decorations up until the 20th century; in the second, a staggering piggy bank showcases the advent of coins across empires, like the Cleopatra VII and Marcus Antonius from 36 BCE and the House of Habsburg mint through the ages; the third is reserved for special exhibitions. When you exit, don't miss the enchanting views over the circular **Lounge** from the alcoves.

EXTRA TIME
A monument of grand proportions, plan at least a half-day roam of the museum's halls across two floors. Or take advantage of the extra time with Thursday late openings from 6pm to 9pm.

TOURS
One-hour guided tours in English take place every Sunday, focusing on the highlights of one collection. An admission ticket is required; tours are an extra cost *(30/60min tour €3/6)*.

★ TOP EXPERIENCE

Naturhistorisches Museum

Nowhere else turns earth science education into an art like the Naturhistorisches Museum Wien. An imperial natural history collection turned colossal exhibit, here you can marvel at minerals, meteorites and moon rock, stand face-to-face with dinosaur giants, walk through human evolution in anthropological displays and see a world of biodiversity preserved.

MAP P36 **B4**

PLANNING TIP
Allow at least two hours for the ground-floor exhibits and extra time for the zoology floor. The museum is closed on Tuesday, but stays open until 8pm Wednesday.

Scan this QR code for opening hours, guided tours and events.

Minerals, Meteorites & Fossils

When you enter the striking dome hall, take the stairs to the right to begin a chronological walk through the mezzanine floor's Earth & Humans exhibit.

Step into the giant chest of geological and geo-cosmic material treasures in **Halls 1–4**, lined with glass cabinets displaying minerals, rocks and gemstones, like the 115kg Swiss glacial smoky quartz (Hall 1), the crystallised branching 'Iron Flowers' from Styria (Hall 2) and a 1000kg mega-cube of rock salt from the Wieliczka salt mine in Poland (Hall 3). The most dazzling exhibit is the Blumenstrauss (flower bouquet), set with 2102 diamonds and 761 precious gemstones, that Maria Theresia gifted to her husband, Emperor Franz I Stephan of Lorraine, in 1760 (Hall 4).

Journey into outer space in **Hall 5**, presenting the world's largest meteorite collection. Among the 1100 out-of-this-world pieces are Martian meteorites like Chassigny, which landed in France in 1815, and a piece of the moon – a fragment of a lunar meteorite found in Mauritius in 2011. On loan from NASA are samples of lunar soil and a piece of basalt rock collected during the Apollo 15 mission in 1971.

Halls 6–9 focus on Planet Earth and Palaeon-tology, showcasing the geological evolution of our

CHLOE POTTER/NHM VIENNA

planet since the Paleozoic Era, some 540 million years ago, through displays of fossils and marine ammonites, including extinct marine arthropod trilobites, molluscs, an oyster reef and the oldest sea snake. The complete skeleton of the prehistoric elephant, Prodeinotherium, is displayed in Hall 9.

Dinosaurs & Prehistoric Finds

Dinosaur buffs should dash to **Hall 10** (pictured). Here stand the skeletons of a diplodocus, iguanodon and the allosaurus, complete with a 6m-long, roaring animatronic replica. Also on display are the skulls of a triceratops and tyrannosaurus rex and the skeleton of an archelon ischyros, the largest turtle ever.

Halls 11 to 13 detail prehistory in artefacts covering Stone Age hunting and Copper Age innovations (Hall 11); a dedicated exhibit on

QUICK BREAK
Grab an imperially sweet *Kaiserschmarrn* to go from the streetside open window at **Demel** (p65), or take a coffee break in the rococo-regency salon cafe upstairs.

Naturhistorisches Museum

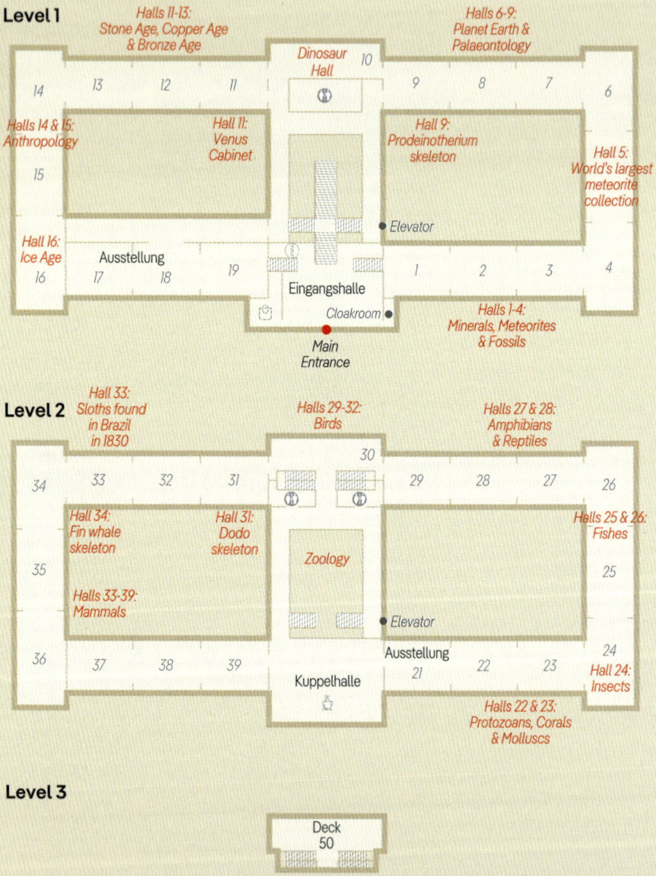

Level 1

Halls 11-13:
Stone Age, Copper Age
& Bronze Age

Halls 6-9:
Planet Earth &
Palaeontology

Dinosaur
Hall

10

14   13   12   11   9   8   7   6

Halls 14 & 15:
Anthropology

Hall 11:
Venus
Cabinet

Hall 9:
Prodeinotherium
skeleton

Hall 5:
World's largest
meteorite
collection

15

Hall 16:
Ice Age

Ausstellung

• *Elevator*

Hall 16:

16   17   18   19   1   2   3   4

Eingangshalle

Cloakroom •

Main
Entrance

Halls 1-4:
Minerals, Meteorites
& Fossils

Level 2

Hall 33:
Sloths found
in Brazil
in 1830

Halls 29-32:
Birds

Halls 27 & 28:
Amphibians
& Reptiles

30

34   33   32   31   29   28   27   26

Hall 34:
Fin whale
skeleton

Hall 31:
Dodo
skeleton

Zoology

Halls 25 & 26:
Fishes

35

Halls 33-39:
Mammals

25

• *Elevator*

Ausstellung

36   37   38   39   21   22   23   24

Kuppelhalle

Hall 24:
Insects

Halls 22 & 23:
Protozoans, Corals
& Molluscs

Level 3

Deck
50

Hallstatt salt mining and burials (Hall 12); and the Late Bronze Age (Hall 13) with the weaponry and armour of Celtic warriors. The prize exhibit here, in a dedicated showroom, is the 29,500-year-old *Venus of Willendorf* Palaeolithic figurine.

Walk through a timeline of human evolution in **Halls 14 and 15**, an anthropological collection dedicated to themes such as brain development and bipedalism, across hands-on stations, reconstructions, skulls and skeletal remains. The ice age focus in **Hall 16** displays ancient animal skeletons, including a 35,000-year-old cave lion.

Zoology

The 2nd floor is entirely devoted to zoology with cabinets of taxidermy and fluid-preserved specimens from single-celled organisms to large mammals; it's a fascinating display of common, endangered and extinct species. At the top of the stairs, turn left to enter the special exhibit Hall 21 to begin.

Halls 22 and 23 spotlight single-cell protozoans, corals and molluscs, featuring a huge Japanese spider crab and a 1.4m-wide giant clam, while **Hall 24** is a creepy-crawly display of flies, beetles, spiders and more. **Halls 25 and 26** have an extinct coelacanth fish among its collection, though the standout amphibians and reptiles in **Halls 27 and 28** are three Galápagos giant tortoises and a Nile crocodile.

Birds fill **Halls 29–32**, including a complete dodo skeleton (Hall 31), moving to a colossal parade of mammals in **Halls 33–39** with show-stopping specimens like the sloths found in 1830 in Brazil (Hall 33), a huge southern elephant seal and a fin whale skeleton (Hall 34), and the now-endangered Javan rhinoceros (Hall 35).

ROOFTOP HIGHS
Rooftop tours take you onto the building's roof to view the ornate architecture up close. English tours *(per person €20)* run at 3pm on Friday, Saturday and Sunday.

A NIGHT AT THE MUSEUM
For the ultimate sleepover, book an overnight **Nacht im Museum** *(per person €110; 7pm-8.30am)* experience, which includes a dinosaur show and torch tour. Children must be accompanied by an adult.

🚶 WALKING TOUR

History Surrounding Stephansplatz

There's a heady mix of architectural styles in the Innere Stadt's streets. Roman history is burrowed beneath the old-trader squares, alleys and hidden courtyards of medieval Vienna, and Modernist designs jostle with dominant baroque facades. Follow a timeline spanning the 13th to the 20th centuries on this landmark walk around iconic St Stephen's Cathedral.

START	END	LENGTH
Stephansplatz	Hoher Markt	3km; 45min

1 Plague Column

The **Graben** is a former Roman moat turned ornate shopping axis. It's dominated by the 21m-high baroque **Pestsäule** (Plague Column), a memorial erected in 1693 following the 1679 plague epidemic.

2 Architecture Misnomer

The functional 1909 residential and retail **Looshaus**, designed by Adolf Loos, caused controversy with its marble-clad mezzanine and unembellished upper levels, breaking the decorative trends of Art Nouveau. It's occupied by the Raiffeisen Bank.

3 Venetian Passage

Enjoy a lavish hit of Italian Renaissance style as you walk through the exquisite Venetian Trecento-style arcade passage of **Palais Ferstel**. It's part of the original 1860 construction for the national bank and stock exchange.

4 12th-Century Squares

Palatial **Am Hof** stands on the grand designs of Duke Heinrich II of Bavaria's square-bound compound of 1154. He commissioned Vienna's oldest monastery church, **Schottenkirche** (Scottish Church), on neighbouring Freyung in 1170. Am Hof was a vendor square in the 13th century, a lineage continued today with festive markets.

5 Old Jewish Quarter

In the old Jewish Quarter, the striking and interpretive concrete **Holocaust memorial**, designed by Rachel Whiteread in 2000, presents an inverted library in a sealed room, alluding to untold stories. It sits on the site of the destroyed 1421 synagogue.

6 Old City Hall

The **Altes Rathaus** (Old City Hall) held city council from 1316, a predecessor of the 1883 Ringstrasse monument. Nearby Ruprechtskirche, from 1200, is the oldest church in Vienna, perched on an elevated weave of cobbled alleys. The Ruprechtsstiege (stairs) chart a pretty route down to the Danube Canal.

7 Hidden Medieval Courtyard

Heiligenkreuzerhof has its foundations in the 1135-founded Heiligenkreuz Abbey. A time-warp passage between Schönlaterngasse and Grashofgasse, today's courtyard was added in 1771 after multiple adaptations. On nearby Griechengasse, the city's oldest restaurant, **Griechenbeisl** (p64), has been serving since 1447.

8 A Square of Ages

The unassuming **Hoher Markt** was a medieval trading hub; earlier, it was part of Roman Vindobona, whose ruins lie beneath in the Römermuseum. Its centrepiece is the *Jugendstil* **Ankeruhr**, a mechanical clock designed by Franz von Matsch in 1911. Figures trundle across the bridge; at noon, they parade to organ music.

WALKING TOUR

Loop the Ringstrasse

The historic centre is chock-full of sites, but a stroll along the Innere Stadt's encompassing 5.3km Ringstrasse (Ring Rd) is a look at the grandiose architectural belt that emerged after the medieval walls were demolished. You'll get to drink third-wave coffee, tour masterwork rooms and, at the right time, stumble upon a city hall festival.

START	END	LENGTH
Österreichische Postsparkasse	Universität Wien	4.3km; 1hr

① Österreichische Postsparkasse

Step inside the sleek, functionalist steel and glass *Jugendstil* (Art Nouveau) bank hall of the **Österreichische Postsparkasse** (Austrian Postal Savings), Otto Wagner's first building commission, realised between 1904 and 1912. Some original counters have been repurposed as creative spaces like the Café Exchange.

② Museum of Applied Arts

The impressive red-brick building with Italian Early Renaissance facade features and columned arcade hall was the Ringstrasse's first museum, built in 1871 for **MAK** (Museum of Applied Arts). Wander exhibits of furniture and other arts and design materials for a socio-historical deep dive into the search for Viennese modern style.

③ Wiener Staatsoper

Behold the **Wiener Staatsoper**, a capsule of Vienna's classical music heritage. It opened in 1869 to Mozart's *Don Giovanni* and has since continued the legacy of the great composers who wrote scores for the stage. The world's largest repertoire of classical music is performed on a daily rotation.

④ The Imperial Complex

The **Neue Burg** was a deliberate architectural plan to assert power by taking a front-row seat on the Ringstrasse. Opposite, the magnum opus of museum complexes was constructed – the **Naturhistorisches Museum** in 1889, followed by the **Kunsthistorisches Museum** two years later. Together they display the Habsburg's extensive treasury of arts and antiquities.

⑤ Österreichisches Parlament

With its Greek temple facade, the **Österreichisches Parlament** (Austrian Parliament) by prominent Ringstrasse architect Theophil von Hansen was emblematic of the political shift from imperial to republic, built in the time of monarchy between 1874 and 1883. Its interactive exhibits and building tours provide an insight into Austrian politics.

⑥ Wiener Rathaus

The spired neo-Gothic-style **Rathaus**, built between 1872 and 1883, was representative of a newly enlarged population. A community pillar, it still sees people gathering on the city hall square opposite the distinguished *Burgtheater* to enjoy festivals, the famed Christmas market and Vienna's Pride Parade.

⑦ Universität Wien

The Italian High Renaissance–designed **Universität Wien** (University of Vienna) opened in 1884 and is home to the oldest university in the German-speaking world, founded in 1365. See the masterwork of Ringstrasse architect Heinrich von Ferstel up close on a guided tour through the Main Ceremonial Chamber and Great Reading Room (in English and German).

EXPERIENCES

Unearth Roman Vindobona
RUINS AND ARTEFACTS

The exposed Roman relics on **Michaelerplatz** (MAP: 1 P36 **D3**) are a sneak peek of Vienna's ancient foundations; the open plot in front of the Hofburg shows the remains of Roman structures thought to have belonged to the entertainment district of the military camp.

The best-preserved ruins of what is believed to be the officers' quarters and some 300 of the 150,000 uncovered artefacts from the legion of Vindobona are housed below Hoher Markt in the

---

HIDDEN CITY WALLS

History fans can find fragments of Vienna's medieval city walls in obscure spaces.

Stubentor U-Bahn
MAP: 3 P36 **H3**

Enter the U3 metro station and find a ticket hall straddled by exposed stone bulks.

Palais Coburg
MAP: 4 P36 **G4**

The luxurious hotel incorporated the foundational relics of the site into its modern reconstruction. The noble family home, built in 1845 upon a bastion, survived the fortification destruction; visitors are free to enter the ground-floor exhibit.

Römermuseum (MAP: 2 P36 **F2**; *Roman Museum; wienmuseum.at/ roemermuseum; adult/child €8/ free)*. The small exhibit includes interactive stations and video displays.

Step into a Medieval Chapel in the U-Bahn
MUSEUM

MAP: 5 P36 **E3**

You might notice the black pavement markings next to Stephansdom denoting where the 800-year-old Mary Magdalene Chapel once stood. Beneath this outline lie the remains of its basement **Virgilkapelle** *(wienmuseum .at/virgilkapelle; adult/child €5/ free),* hidden for centuries before its discovery in 1973 during the metro construction.

Entrance to the site is located within the Stephansplatz U-Bahn station; a winding staircase leads down to the preserved 13th-century vaulted interior ruins. Its story is explained in the tiny multimedia and artefact-dotted exhibit on medieval Vienna.

Admire the Palace of Justice's Interiors
ARCHITECTURE

MAP: 6 P36 **A4**

The **Justizpalast** *(Palace of Justice; admission free)* is more than a grandiose facade. Inside, the impressive Renaissance-style interior courtyard has two-tiered arcades and an impressive staircase, presided over by the statue of *grande dame* Justitia (Lady Justice). This is a reconstruction of the 1875 original, rebuilt after the building was set ablaze during a protest by Social Democratic workers in 1927.

As the seat of Austria's Supreme Court, entry is limited. Between 9.30am and 3.30pm Monday to Friday, only 25 people are granted admission per hour, subject to security screening; last entry is at 2.30pm. The rooftop **Justizcafé** overlooks Parliament, with views to the Rathaus and Votivkirche.

Remember Jewish Vienna MUSEUM

Vienna's Jewish history goes back to the Middle Ages, but by 1945 only 5000 of its 180,000 members had survived the Holocaust. The **Jüdisches Museum** (MAP: ⑦ P36 E3; *jmw.at; adult/child €15/free)* encourages dialogue about the road to reconciliation. Its split collection – 1945 to the present day and the Middle Ages to the Shoah – elucidates varied perspectives on identity, persecution and present-day Judaism in the capital, while temporary exhibitions often tackle more controversial topics.

Its second branch, **Museum Judenplatz** (MAP: ⑧ P36 E1), built around the on-show excavations of the destroyed synagogue of 1421 by the order of Duke Albert V, is an interactive station and visual tour of the city's medieval Jewry. Tickets allow entry to both museums and are valid for seven days.

Experience Virtual Reality Vienna INTERACTIVE EXHIBIT

MAP: ⑨ P36 D3

Time Travel Vienna (*timetravel-vienna.at; adult/child €21.85/18.05*) takes you on a standing, spinning and soaring interactive and multimedia journey through the history of the city, with virtual reality headsets, animatronic wax figures that bring the Habsburgs to life, themed rooms and a 5D *Fiaker* (carriage) ride.

Across the road, **Sisi's Amazing Journey** (*amazing-sisi.at; adult/child €11.40/8.55*) takes you on a 5D ride below and above ground. A combo ticket with Time Travel Vienna costs adult/child €28/24.

Browse National Library Treasures MUSEUMS

Aside from the show-stopping Prunksaal, the **Austrian National Library** has a collection of permanent exhibitions, the most notable among them the world's only **Globenmuseum** (MAP. ⑩ P36 C2; Globe Museum; *onb.ac.at/en/museums/globe-museum; adult/child €6/free)*. The Palais Mollard holds a staggering 250 pre-1850 geographical and landscape-detail terrestrial globes, alongside planetary and stargazing celestial spheres showcasing cartographic and cosmological science, including the adorned treasures gifted to emperors over the ages. In the same building, the small **Esperantomuseum** (see ⑩) is dedicated to artificial language and is included in the ticket.

While the ancient paper displays of the **Papyrusmuseum** (MAP: ⑪ P36 **C4**; *onb.ac.at/en/museums/papyrus-museum; adult/child €6/free*) can be found in the Neue Burg, this compact exhibit's treasure is the oldest object of the library – the 3400-year-old Egyptian papyrus *Book of the Dead of Sesostris*.

Get an Alternative Perspective
WALKING TOURS

Hear the lesser-known legends behind the centuries-old hidden courtyards and cobblestoned laneways on the 'Hidden Vienna' walking tour offered by **Rebel Tours** (*rebeltoursvienna.com; adult/child €35/15*). Or consider joining an early morning 1½-hour running tour between grand monuments.

Cold War–era secrets are revealed on the 'I Spy Vienna' tour by **Hidden Vienna** (*hiddenvienna.guide; adult/child €35/27*) with stories of espionage from the 1st district's quadrant Inter-Allied Zone. Or learn about the struggle for survival on its streets and slums during Imperial times on the 'Gangs of Vienna' option.

The city might be known for its boundless beauty, but Eugene Quinn from **Whoosh** (*whoosh.wien; adult/child €10/free*) shows the controversial and rebellious architectural misfits on his tongue-in-cheek 'Vienna Ugly Tour'.

You'll learn about the polarising, often unseen sides of the city with **Shades Tours** (*shades-tours.com; up to 15 people €234*) – walks led by those affected by homelessness and addiction, and for whom a job as a guide is a chance to rebuild their lives. Only private tours are available in English.

See Vienna on Wheels
BIKE AND MOTOR TOURS

Those with a need for speed can set off in a single-seater, pocket-rocket motor car with **Hotrod Tour Wein** (MAP: ⑫ P36 **F2**; *hotrod-tour.at; per person €150*), circuiting the city in convoy on a 1½-hour spin around the

---

 THE STORY OF SACHER TORTE

No trip to Vienna is complete without sampling a slice of **Sacher Torte** – fondant-iced chocolate sponge cake with a layer of apricot jam, served with *Schlagobers* (whipped cream). Pâtissier Franz Sacher created the *Sacher Torte* in 1832 for Prince Klemens Wenzel von Metternich. Sacher's son, Eduard, refined the recipe when apprenticing at the court confectioner Demel, before opening the Sacher Hotel in 1876. Legal battles raged between Demel and Café Sacher over the recipe and trademark. An out-of-court settlement in 1963 granted Café Sacher the rights to the name 'Original Sacher Torte', and Demel to use a decorative triangular seal reading 'Eduard-Sacher-Torte'.

architectural conveyor belt Ring-strasse and through historic centre alleys. A valid class B driving licence is required.

Alternatively, bike the boulevards on a Classic Vienna Bike Tour with **Pedal Power** (MAP: 13 P36 E6; *pedalpower.at; €47*). On a leisurely three-hour wheel you'll take in the city's highlights.

Watch the Wiener Philharmoniker Perform
CONCERT HALL

MAP: 14 P36 F6

The prestigious **Musikverein** *(music society; musikverein.at; standing/seated tickets from €19/69)* opened its doors in 1870. Its most famed hall, the gilded cuboid Goldener Saal (Golden Hall), is the permanent home of the Wiener Philharmoniker (Vienna Philharmonic Orchestra), whose sell-out New Year's Concert is broadcast globally from here. The architectural acoustic wonder holds an audience of 2000, overlooked by Apollo and the Nine Muses on its frescoed ceiling. Regular **Mozart Concerts**, performed in historical costumes, resound here.

Daily 45-minute **tours** *(€10)* take you behind the scenes of this remarkable building Monday to Saturday.

Enjoy Classical Castle Performances
CONCERT HALL

MAP: 16 P36 C4

In the Hofburg's Neue Burg wing, the neoclassical imperial ballroom

WORLD-FAMOUS OPERA

MAP: 15 P36 E5

An evening at the **Wiener Staatsoper** (Vienna State Opera; *wiener-staatsoper.at*), which stages around 50 operas and Vienna State Ballet productions per season, is a quintessential Viennese experience. Regular tickets can be purchased two months in advance and cost between €18 and €295. Buy online or wait in the queue to bag cheaper tickets at the standing-room box office on Operngasse (available 80 minutes before the performance; up to €18).

Beyond performances, daily guided tours *(adult/child €15/9)* wind from the luxurious foyer and staircase, through the plush auditorium levels and into the opulent state rooms that survived wartime damage. Book online or at the ticket office 30 minutes before the tour.

Zeremoniensaal (Ceremonial Hall), with its marble columns and chandeliers, is the home of the **Vienna Hofburg Orchestra** *(hofburgorchester.at),* established in 1971 as a collective of classical musicians from all of the capital's major orchestras.

Between May and October, they perform their signature Strauss and Mozart concert here, accompanied by singers and ballet soloists from the city's opera stages. Performances start at 8.30pm; tickets *(from €45)* are available online. There is no fixed seating so arrive early to secure a good position.

The sumptuous *Festsaal* (Great Hall), with frescoed ceiling panels and lunettes, is used for the Christmas and New Year's concerts.

Explore the House of Sound

MUSIC MUSEUM

MAP: 17 P36 F5

The four-floored **Haus der Musik** *(hdm.at; adult/child €17/7)* museum is a multisensory classical-music schooling, starting with a melodic staircase entrance.

The archive-filled 1st floor is dedicated to the Wiener Philharmoniker – its founder, conductor and composer Otto Nicolai lived here from 1841 to 1847.

Before moving between the visual thwack of rooms playing the symphonic scores of each of the six Great Masters, learn about the science of sounds in the 2nd-floor interactive Sonotopia laboratory. At the end, you'll pick up a conducting baton and test your skills on the Virtual Conductor, cueing the Philharmonic Orchestra in the Golden Hall of the Vienna Musikverein.

Get to Know Mozart in Vienna

HOUSE MUSEUM & MULTIMEDIA EXHIBIT

Mozart changed addresses 13 times; his most successful years were spent at Domgasse 5 – the only apartment still standing. Navigate three exhibit floors of **Mozarthaus Vienna** (MAP: 18 P36 F3; *mozarthaus vienna.at; adult/child €14/4.50)* with the free one-hour audio guide, starting with the composer's arrival in Vienna in 1781, moving through his musical repertoire, notably *The Marriage of Figaro*, which he wrote here, and ending at the apartment on the 1st floor where he lived for 2½ years between 1784 and 1787. Special attention is given to highlighting original decor and placing a period object in each of the seven rooms to bring the 18th-century grandeur to life.

When Mozart died in 1791, aged 35, he was living on Rauhensteingasse 8, where the Steffl Department Store now stands. In its lower level, the **Mythos Mozart** (MAP: 19 P36 E4; *mythos-mozart.com; adult/child €23/12)* exhibition presents a timeline of his life through a multimedia melody across five fantastical rooms.

Visit Beethoven Abodes

HOUSE MUSEUMS

MAP: 20 P36 B1

Beethoven changed his address in Vienna more than any other composer, but the Pasqualati family kept their 4th-floor apartment for him. The **Beethoven Pasqualati-haus** *(wienmuseum.at/beethoven _pasqualatihaus; adult/child €5/ free)* museum focuses on his eight years here, where he composed three of his nine symphonies and his only opera, *Fidelio*.

A bit further out and north of the centre, the 19th district's

Beethoven Museum *(wien museum.at/beethoven_museum; adult/child €8/free)* offers a broader account of his life's work. Among the displays are his piano and a lock of hair.

Join the Creative Music Scene
JAZZ CLUB

MAP: **21** P36 **G3**

Vienna's creative basement jazz and music club fixture, **Porgy & Bess** *(porgy.at)* stages European and international talent. Velvety and dimly lit, this is an intimate space for the meeting of expressive artists. With a capacity of just 350, it's best to book ahead for popular acts.

Be Dazzled by the Christkindlmarkt
CHRISTMAS MARKET

MAP: **22** P36 **B2**

The biggest and best-known Advent market, the **Wiener Christkindlmarkt am Rathausplatz** fills the square between the Gothic *Rathaus* (city hall) and the neo-Baroque *Burgtheater* with a 'Christmas Dream' themed wonderland. Ride a vintage carousel, browse 120 festive huts and visit the gardens decorated with dazzling light displays, illuminated pathways and a loop-lane ice rink.

Take a Look at the Klimt-led Art Movement
CONTEMPORARY ART HALL

MAP: **23** P36 **D6**

The **Secession** *(secession.at; adult/child €12/free)* exhibition space was founded in 1897 by the Klimt-led visual artist collective. The white-cubed building topped by a gold dome of 3000 gold-plated laurel leaves is Vienna's *Jugendstil* symbol and the world's oldest independent exhibition hall dedicated to contemporary art.

Its permanent display is from the movement's 14th exhibition in 1901, in tribute to Beethoven on the 75th anniversary of his death – the monumental work of Klimt's *Beethovenfries* (Beethoven Frieze) depicting the search for happiness. Today's viewing is a multisensory experience, observing the painted wall while the composer's *Symphony No 9 in D Minor* plays through headphones.

Gaze at Contemporary Austrian Art
ART GALLERY

MAP: **24** P36 **E6**

One of the city's newer galleries and the contemporary sister of the Albertina, the **Albertina Modern** *(albertina.at/albertina modern; adult/child €15.90/free)* counts over 60,000 contemporary works of Austrian artists such as Hermann Nitsch, Maria Lassnig and Friedensreich Hundertwasser and international greats like Andy Warhol in its rotating collection. Displays fill the Künstlerhaus building, restoring the 1868 architectural monument near the Ringstrasse that Emperor Franz Joseph I commissioned as an exhibition space for the city's artists.

LISTINGS

Best Places for...

G Budget   **GG** Midrange   **GGG** Top End

See p36 for map of locations

Eating

Schnitzel

Figlmüller at Wollzeile **GG**

25 F2

A tourist magnet it may be, but Figlmüller does have legendary status. This famous restaurant has been serving some of the biggest and best schnitzels in the business for over 115 years. *11am-10.30pm*

Meissl & Schadn **GGG**

26 G6

Hip restaurant of the Grand Hotel Ferdinand, taking you on a culinary journey of the *Wiener Schnitzel*. Before feasting, watch how it's perfectly beaten and baked through the open salon kitchen in front of the restaurant. *11.30am-11pm*

Gasthaus zur Oper **GG**

27 E5

The contemporary venue of the classic culinary institution and *Tafel-spitz*-famed (boiled beef)

Plachutta. It serves a perfectly prepared house recipe *Wiener Schnitzel. 11.30am-midnight*

Historic Establishments

Griechenbeisl **GG**

28 G2

Feast on *Wiener Schnitzel* (breadcrumbed veal cutlet) and *Kaiserschmarrn* (sweet pancake) in the city's oldest *Beisl*. The signature wall in the Mark Twain Zimmer (room) features the scribbles of famous guests. *noon-11pm*

Zwölf Apostelkeller **GG**

29 G2

Old-fashioned restaurant in a Romanesque and Gothic period cellar. Serves Austrian classics, smoked meats and suckling pig, Austrian wine, beer and schnapps, with traditional *Heuriger* (wine tavern) ballads daily from 7pm. *11am-midnight*

Esterhazykeller **GG**

30 D2

Tucked in a quiet courtyard off Kohlmarkt, this 15th-century rustic cellar has served wine

since 1683. Today, it offers Esterházy Palace estate wines, alongside beer and spirits. Dig into Austrian classics at the adjoining Stüberl restaurant. *11am-10pm*

Contemporary Austrian

Motto am Fluss **GG**

31 G1

Cosmopolitan cafe and restaurant in a canal-anchored boat serving contemporary Austrian-international cuisine against views of the Danube Canal. *6pm-11pm Mon-Sat, to 10.30pm Sun, bar to midnight*

Die Cafetière **GG**

32 D1

Revived mid-century modern cafe and purveyors of the tastiest Viennese cheese and ham toastie. *7.20am-6pm Mon-Fri, 9am-4pm Sat*

Vegetarian

Wrenkh **GG**

33 F2

This bistro specialises exclusively in dishes made with seasonal vegetables, from potato goulash and mushroom schnitzel to tom yam fennel. A two- to three-course lunch menu is served until 3pm. *11am-11pm Mon-Fri, from noon-11pm Sat*

Tian

 F4

Michelin-starred gourmet vegetarian restaurant rooted in rare ingredients and experimental cooking. A set six- to eight-course menu is served, with optional wine pairing. Book at least a month in advance. *6am-11pm Tue-Sat*

Drinking

Coffee Houses

Café Central

 C2

This queue-commanding, vaulted, marble and gilded coffee house was the elite meeting place of poets, philosophers and revolutionaries. There are daily piano music performances from 4.30pm to 9.30pm. *8am-10pm Mon-Sat, from 10am Sun*

Demel

 D3

The former imperial suppliers have served artisanal delicacies since 1786. Sample its

Eduard-Sacher-Torte in the graceful rococo-regency salon cafe upstairs. *10am-7pm*

Café Sacher

 E5

This option still has the air of high society, though it's most celebrated for its chocolate fondant cake with apricot jam, best served with a *Wiener Melange* (coffee with milk foam). *7am-11pm*

Café Hawelka

 E3

A family-run city institution since 1939, known for its lounge-worthy late nights and servings of jam-filled *Buchteln* (sweet rolls), made with a family recipe. *9am-midnight Mon-Thu, to 1am Fri & Sat, 10am-9pm Sun*

Kaffee Alt Wien

 G2

The poster-plastered, dusky predecessor of Café Hawelka. Its late-night opening hours meld the vibes of coffee house and hip pub. *10am-midnight Mon-Wed & Sun, to 1am Thu, to 2am Fri*

Café Prückel

 H3

Light and airy pastel-hued beauty from 1903 that's an icon of Art Nouveau style on the Ringstrasse, opposite the

Museum of Applied Arts. *8.30am-10pm*

Café Landtmann

 B1

Freud's favourite, this polished place continues to serve coffee-house culture to international patrons as it did when it opened in 1873 for the Vienna World's Fair. *7.30am-11pm*

Café Schwarzenberg

 F6

Wood-clad, marble-mirrored time capsule from 1861 that's the oldest Ringstrasse cafe. Hosts live jazz music sessions every Sunday. *7.30am-11.30pm Mon-Fri, from 8.30am Sat & Sun*

Café Korb

 E2

A 1904 cafe turned colourful, art-splashed lounge, blending its 1960s era remodelling with red velvet booths and glass light shades. Puts on live music concerts. *8am-midnight Sat & Sun*

Cafes

Kleines Café

 F4

This tiny 48-seat bohemian hangout, designed by architect Hermann Czech in the 1970s, spills outside onto a cobblestoned square. *10am-2am*

Parémi

45 G3

Delectable French bakery combining impeccable coffee with Vienna's finest croissants and patisserie sweet treats. It's also a beautiful lunch spot with sandwiches, salads and quiches. *7.30am-6pm Tue-Sat*

Guesthouse Brasserie & Bakery

46 E4

All-day establishment melding traditional Austrian and French cuisine, including seafood options like oysters and moules-frites. It has two-course weekday lunch specials for €24. *6.30am-midnight*

Cocktail Bars

Dino's Apothecary Bar

47 E1

A dark wood-panelled, low-light, classic cocktail bar with an extensive experimental menu. *5pm-2am Tue-Thu, to 3am Fri & Sat*

Loos American Bar

48 E3

Celeb magnet and cult status Art Deco bar designed by Viennese Modernism architect Adolf Loos, decked in marble, mirror and mahogany. Daily champagne specials are served between noon and 4pm. *noon-4am*

Kleinod Prunkstück

49 F2

Chic, low-lit, late-night cocktail joint with mirror-ceiling bar, dark-wood trims and plush banquettes. *6pm-2am Sun-Wed, to 4am Thu-Sat*

Needle Vinyl Bar

50 D1

A trendy, retro-styled, record-spinning bar lounge, mixing music and signature cocktails. *5pm-2am*

Rooftop Bars

Lamée Rooftop Bar

51 F2

The chic rooftop bar of Hotel Topazz Lamée has one of the best views of Stephansdom. *11am-1am Sun-Thu, to 2am Fri & Sat*

Atmosphere Rooftop Bar

52 G5

The roof terrace bar of the Ritz-Carlton hotel hosts seasonal events against a sweeping city view. *4-10.30pm*

Sky Bar im Steffl

53 E4

Shopping mile Kärntner Strasse's Steffl department store has a rooftop bar and garden overlooking Stephansdom. *10am-midnight*

Craft Beer

1516 Brewing Company

54 F5

This two-level brewpub is always bustling, partly due to its late-night kitchen (spanning burgers to schnitzel) but also for its craft tap beer with seasonal specials. *10am-2am*

Mel's Craft Beers & Diner

55 E1

With over 25 craft beers and ciders on tap, start with the six-sample tasting rack. Or choose from over 100 Austrian and European bottled brews. Food and beer combo specials run Monday to Friday until 4pm. *11am-midnight*

Shopping

Imperial Legacy Stores

J&L Lobmeyr

56 E4

Glittering displays of fine crystal and glassware fill marble-columned, chandeliered floors. It's one of Vienna's most lavish retail experiences on Kärntner Strasse, operating since 1823 when it exclusively supplied the imperial court. *10am-6pm Mon-Sat*

Gerstner

57 E5

The imperial sweet suppliers from 1847, Gerstner's gilded confectionery foyer brims with cakes, pastries, delectable works of art and unique chocolate bars with Viennese flavours. *8am-10pm*

Augarten Wien

58 E3

If you can't make it to the factory site, this flagship store of the capital's porcelain manufacturer Augarten sells the most delicate of ornaments and dinnerware with traditional hand-painted designs. *10am-6pm Mon-Sat*

Rozet und Fischmeister

59 D3

Founded in 1770, these imperial jewellers use time-honoured techniques to craft exquisite, princely priced pieces, along with silverware. *11am-6pm Mon-Fri, 10.30am-3pm Sat*

Viennese Souvenirs

Zuckerlwerkstatt

60 E4

Marvel at Vienna's 150-year-old candy

craftsmanship in this open workshop. The store is stacked with jars of striped candies, roller sweets and fruit jellies, all made with natural ingredients. *10am-6pm Mon-Sat*

Wiener Seife

61 D2

These plant-oil-based handmade soaps are still made to an old secret recipe. Sisi Violet, Viennese Rose, Viennese Scent and Blue Danube are the classic fragrances. *10am-6.30pm Mon-Fri, to 6pm Sat*

Manner

62 F2

Sweetening the city since 1889, Manner's salmon-pink brand colour is instantly recognisable. The Original Neapolitaner (hazelnut wafer) is the mainstay, but inside the store you'll find chocolate-coated morsels and merch. *10am-9pm*

Hamtil & Söhne

63 D3

Mass-produced trinkets are out. Here you'll find design-led souvenirs, many of which are crafted in the city, from books and beverages, homewares to original *Wiener*

Achtelgläser (wine tavern glasses). *10am-7pm*

Delicacies

Theehandlung Schönbichler

64 F3

Master tea blenders since 1870. Choose your infusion or create your own in this *Apotheke*-like setup with gilt scales and wood-panelled shelves stocked with black jars. *9am-5pm Mon-Fri, to 6.30pm Sat*

Julius Meinl am Graben

65 D2

Since 1862, Vienna's gourmet store has overflowed with international delicacies: the ground floor with confectionery, upstairs with cheeses and meats. Meinl's Café Bar serves fine wines and coffee. *8am-7.30pm Mon-Fri, 9am-6pm Sat*

Xocolat

66 C2

Speciality shop with beautifully decorated handmade chocolates, pralines, truffles and handcrafted bars. With stores around the city, the exemplary Ferstel Passage branch was where it all started. *10am-6pm Mon-Sat*

See p80

for eating, drinking and shopping listings

Explore
Prater & Around: Leopoldstadt

The vibrant urban wedge between the waters of the bar-lined Danube Canal (Donaukanal) and the Danube (Donau) River is the 2nd district, Leopoldstadt – the former Jewish quarter turned hip 'hood that remains multicultural at heart. Prater Park's greenery stretches 3000 acres through the district, a city oasis home to the Wurstelprater amusement park and the Wiener Riesenrad icon. The baroque gardens of Augarten, juxtaposed with the wartime concrete *Flaktürme* (flak towers) and the trendy Karmelitermarkt, complete the trio of stop-ins. Bar- and cafe-lined Taborstrasse and Praterstrasse connect the green spaces to the centre via the canal.

Getting Around

 Walk

The 2nd district's Danube Canal stretch can be reached by the short Schwedenbrücke (bridge) from the 1st district fringe, Schwedenplatz. Karmelitermarkt is a 10-minute walk from the canal.

U U-Bahn (Metro)

Schwedenplatz U-Bahn (U1 and U4 lines) is closest to the Danube Canal, Taborstrasse (U2) for Karmelitermarkt, Praterstern (U1 and U2) for the Wurstelprater, and Vorgartenstrasse (U1) for the Stuwerviertel neighbourhood.

Tram

Tram lines 0 and 5 go to Wurstelprater. Lines 2 and 5 go to Augarten (the closest stop is Am Tabor).

Karmeliterviertel (p79)

THE BEST

GREEN PARK
Prater Park (p72)

VIEWPOINT
Wiener Riesenrad (p72)

WATERSIDE BARS
Danube Canal (p78)

UNUSUAL SITE
Flaktürme in Augarten (p78)

NEIGHBOURHOOD
Karmeliterviertel (p79)

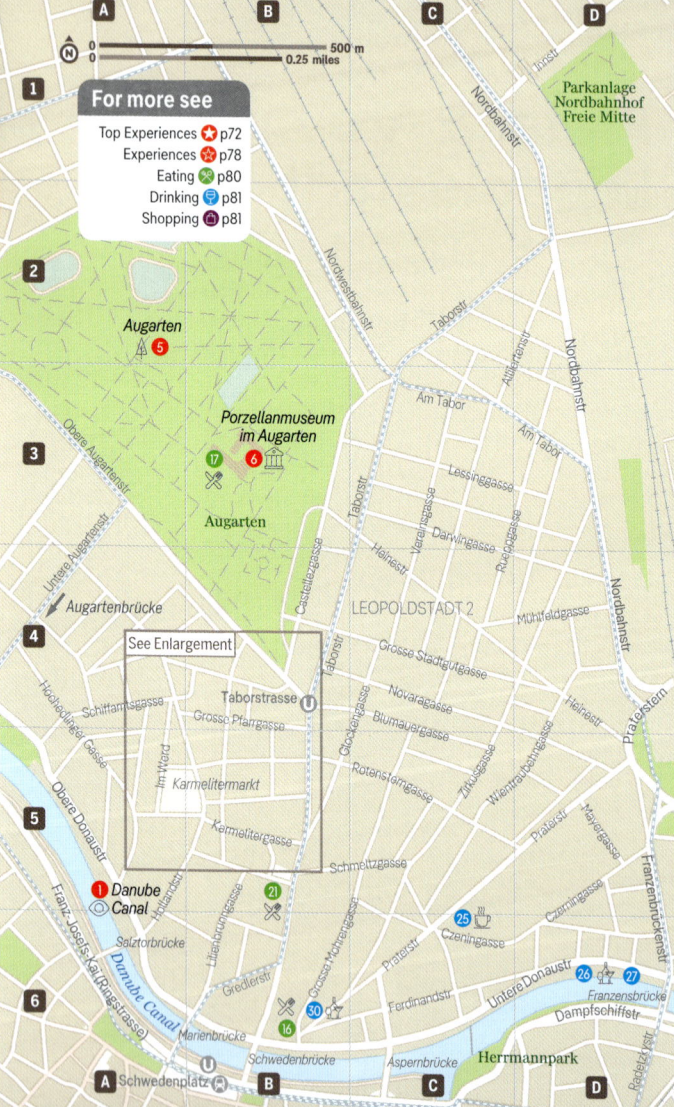

For more see

Top Experiences	p72
Experiences	p78
Eating	p80
Drinking	p81
Shopping	p81

Parkanlage
Nordbahnhof
Freie Mitte

Augarten

Porzellanmuseum
im Augarten

Augarten

LEOPOLDSTADT 2

Augartenbrücke

See Enlargement

Taborstrasse

Grosse Pfarrgasse

Karmelitermarkt

Karmelitergasse

Danube
Canal

Herrmannpark

Franzensbrücke
Dampfschiffstr

Schwedenplatz

Neue Donau

Donauinsel

Donauinsel

Reichsbrücke

Danube

Handelskai

Erzherzogstr

Augarten

Das MuTh

Obere Augartenstr

Kleine Pfarrgasse

Schiffamtsgasse

Taborstrasse

Grosse Pfarrgasse

Leopoldsgasse

Grosse Sperlgasse

Grosse Schiffgasse

Im Werd

Haidgasse

LEOPOLDSTADT 2

Tandelmarktgasse

Karmelitermarkt

Karmelitergasse

Taborstr

Holfandstr

Karmeliterviertel

Karmeliterplatz

0   100 m

Lessing-Roth-Gasse

Lassallestr

Vorgartenmarkt

Ybbsstr

Wohnstr

Engerthstr

Vorgartenstr

Lassallestr

Engerthstr

Max-Winter-Park

Stuwerviertel

Wolfgang-Schmälzl-Gasse

Venediger-Au-Gasse

Obermüllerstr

Venediger-Au-Park

Max Winter Str

Stuwerstr

Praterstern

Ausstellungsstr

Messe Prater

Ausstellungsstr

Wien Nord

Ausstellungsstr

Nordportalstr

Wurstelprater

Prater Museum

Wiener Riesenrad

Liliputbahn

Str des Ersten Mai

Prater Turm

Zufahrtsstr

Nordportalstr

Südportalstr

Wirtschaftsuniversität

Prater

Hauptallee

Prater Park

Vivariumstr

Eduard-Lang-Weg

Waldsteingartenstr

Unterer Prater Fasangarten

Schüttelstr

Laufbergergasse

Böcklinstr

Sportklubstr

Hauptallee

⭐ **TOP EXPERIENCE**

Prater Park

Vienna's green spaces go beyond palace gardens and city parks, and the 2nd district delivers. To get acquainted with Prater, first know that it's typically referred to in two parts: the recreational city escape of Prater, formed when Emperor Joseph II opened the imperial hunting grounds to the public in 1766, and the supercharged Wurstelprater fairground with over 200 attractions.

MAP P70 **F6**

PLANNING TIP
The park is busiest on weekends and public holidays when locals make the most of it. Consider visiting on weekdays to avoid the crowds. Attractions open between 11am to midnight.

Scan this QR code for the attractions and opening hours.

Vienna Giant Ferris Wheel

The Rotunda may no longer stand, but the **Wiener Riesenrad** (Vienna Giant Ferris Wheel; *wienerriesenrad.com; adult/child €14.50/6.50*) remains a firm fixture.

The landmark of the park since 1897, the original 30-gondola structure was built in celebration of the Golden Jubilee of Emperor Franz Joseph I and was the largest of its time. So beloved, it was part of a trio of structures alongside Stephansdom and the Vienna State Opera, rebuilt following extensive damage during WWII and given cinematic fame in *The Third Man* (1949), James Bond's *The Living Daylights* (1987) and *Before Sunrise* (1995).

Today a turn in one of its 15 iconic red rectangular wagons circles you almost 65m above Vienna for a prime Danube-side view over the city and its green basin – it's a 15-minute journey with audio commentary. Eight obsolete cabins were turned into exhibits in the **Wheel of History** audiovisual panorama museum; the wheel ticket includes entry.

KARIMJARMOUNI/SHUTTERSTOCK

Prater Tower

The fairground has high-speed spinners like the 100km/h Turbo Booster, a 85m free-falling dropper and hair-raising coasters, but the **Prater Turm** (Prater Tower; *€10;* pictured above) is the highlight – an old-time metal swing carousel twirls 117m up the axis at a wind-whirling velocity of 60km/h.

You don't get expansive views, but you do get a terrific look at the span of Prater from its highest attraction.

Park History at the Prater Museum

Prater was the site for the Vienna World's Fair in 1873. Aside from countless country pavilions, its showpiece Rotunda was the largest domed construction in the world; it burned down in 1937.

Opened in 2023, the **Prater Museum** (*wienmuseum.at/pratermuseum; 11am-6pm Tue-Sun; adult/child €8/free*) revives the history

QUICK BREAK
Take a pit stop in Prater's traditional beer garden, **Schweizerhaus**, serving brews since 1766. It's renowned for its traditional speciality – the giant, crispy pork knuckle.

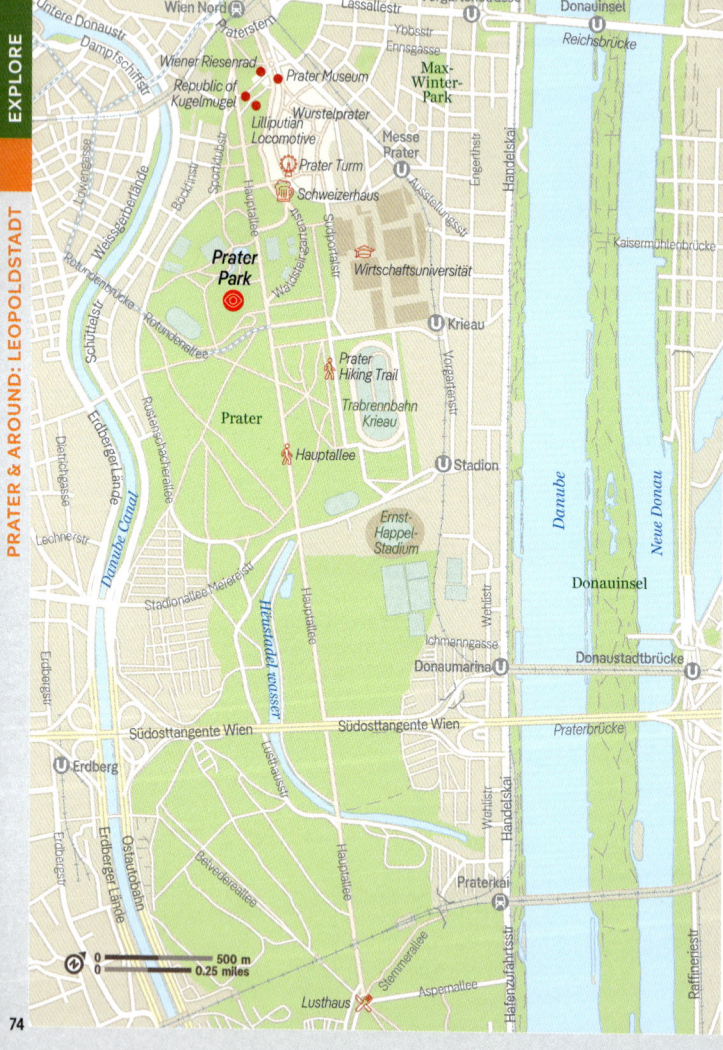

Praterstr
Praterstern
Wien Nord
Praterstern
Lassallestr
Vorgartenstrasse
Donauinsel
Untere Donaustr
Damp tschiffstr
Reichsbrücke
Ybbsstr
Ennisgasse
Wiener Riesenrad
Prater Museum
Max-Winter-Park
Republic of Kugelmugel
Prater Museum
Wurstelprater
Lilliputian Locomotive
Messe Prater
Prater Turm
Engerthstr
Handelskai
Schweizerhaus
Ausstellungsstr
Kaisermühlenbrücke
Prater Park
Wirtschaftsuniversität
Waldsteing
Sportplatzg
Hauptallee
Krieau
Rotundenbrücke
Rotundenallee
Prater Hiking Trail
Vorgartenstr
Schüttelstr
Rustenschacherallee
Prater
Trabrennbahn Krieau
Danube
Neue Donau
Dietrichgasse
Lechnerstr
Hauptallee
Stadion
Ernst-Happel-Stadium
Donauinsel
Danube Canal
Erdbergär Lände
Stadionallee Meiereistr
Heustadel wasser
Ichmanngasse
Donaustadtbrücke
Donaumarina
Hauptallee
Wehlistr
Handelskai
Südosttangente Wien
Südosttangente Wien
Praterbrücke
Erdberg
Lustallee
Wiehtstr
Erdberger Lände
Belvedereallee
Ostautobahn
Hauptallee
Praterkai
Erdberggasse
Stemmeallee
Hafenzufahrtsstr
Raffineriestr
0   500 m
0   0.25 miles
Lusthaus
Aspernallee

74

of the amusement park in a three-storey wooden building. The park's 250-year timeline is told through scale models, historic sculptures and puppets, vintage arcade machines and former ride relics, photography, posters and park materials.

The Lilliputian Locomotive

The **Lilliputian Locomotive** (*liliswelt.at; round trip adult/child €6/3.50*) has been trundling a 4km loop between the Ferris Wheel and the green Prater forests since 1928 and is a rite of passage for all visitors.

The nearly 60-year-old diesel locomotive is today's main runner while the 90-year-old historic steam locomotive is pulled out for the big events. In 20 minutes, you get a scenic introduction – and easier access across four stations – to a large swath of the park. It operates from March to November.

Green Highway: Hauptallee

Covering 6 million sq metres, the expanse of Prater can seem daunting to explore, but the 4.5km-long tree-lined **Hauptallee** (Main Ave) cutting straight through it is the best way to enjoy it without getting lost. You can walk from Wurstelprater to the path's end at the former imperial hunting lodge turned classic Lusthaus restaurant in around one hour.

Along the way, you'll pass the **Republic of Kugelmugel**, declared a 'micronation' by its artist creator to save it from demolition. It's now a (sporadically open) gallery space in the park.

The Prater Hiking Trail

Ramblers can get off the main path. Of the 14 **Wiener Stadtwanderwege** (Vienna city walking trails), one is a well-marked 13km loop through woodland in the Prater, getting you into more dense and serene pockets but without being completely isolated. Look for the wooden signposts etched with 'Stadtwanderweg 9'.

CASH ONLY
The amusement park doesn't work on a single-entry ticket with unlimited attraction access. It's a pay-per-ride system and predominantly cash only. Most attractions cost between €3.50 and €6.

DESIGN CAMPUS
Architecture enthusiasts can admire the Zaha Hadid–designed Library & Learning Centre of the neighbouring **Wirtschaftsuniversität** (Business University) campus, accessible from the U2 Messe-Prater station.

WALKING TOUR

Leopoldstadt: Monuments & Meadows

Walk between the city's oldest hotel, legacy theatre district and Strauss' Blue Danube home, find naval monuments and restored steamships, and end at a Buddhist pagoda. Passing waterfronts and swathes of green, this urban-to-nature trail takes you through Leopoldstadt's layered past, touching upon the imperial and the artistic, the quirky and the lesser known.

START	END	LENGTH
Hotel Stefanie	Vienna Peace Pagoda	7.5km; 1hr 40min

① Vienna's Oldest Hotel

It started out as an inn for travellers in 1600 then became one of the city's largest hotels during the Vienna World's Fair in 1873. In 1881 it was renamed **Hotel Stefanie** to commemorate the wedding of Crown Prince Rudolf and Princess Stephanie of Belgium. Inside is an antique showcase of clocks and porcelain, and an impressive collection of imperial-era army uniforms and royal commemorative memorabilia.

② District Theatre Legacy

Connect to Praterstrasse at the cafe-lined **Nestroyplatz**, the eponymous square ornamented with a statue of satirical playwright Johann Nestroy, honouring Leopoldstadt's 19th-century theatre boom. The **Nestroyhof** building stands opposite the first stage, the Leopoldstadt Theatre (later the Carltheater), destroyed in 1944. The legacy lives on in the district's pocket of performing arts venues and historic cinemas.

③ River Inspiring Strauss House

At Praterstrasse 54, step into the home where the exalted anthem of Vienna, the *Blue Danube Waltz*, was created in 1867. The **Johann Strauss Wohnung** (apartment) is a commemorative museum that, among its displays, includes the Waltz King's violin, baby grand piano and harmonium.

④ Navel Victory Monument

At Praterstern, you'll find the 11m-high marble **Tegetthoff-Denkmal**. The memorial column was erected in 1871 upon the death of the Austro-Hungarian naval hero Admiral Wilhelm von Tegetthoff, sculpted with bronze ship bows and topped with a statue of the supreme commander.

⑤ Imperial Party Pavilion

Take a one-hour stroll along tree-lined Hauptallee to get to the **Lusthaus**. This was the base for imperial hunting parties until the 18th century, when the Prater was opened to the public. An octagonal pavilion, built some 20 years later in 1783, hosted military generals. Today's cafe-restaurant occupies the space restored after WWII damage.

⑥ Emperor Franz Joseph's Secret Ship

On the River Danube, a collection of restored historic steamers has been turned into a **Schiffmuseum** (ship museum) by Captain Franz Scheriau. One remains as inconspicuous as it was intended. The MS *Frédéric Mistral* was a secret vessel used by Emperor Franz Joseph I; you can take a look inside the 'Emperor's Cabin' in the ship's bow.

⑦ Vienna Peace Pagoda

Enjoy a moment of Zen at the end of the route. The **Vienna Peace Pagoda** sits tranquilly on the banks of the Danube among fluttering prayer flags next to the low-key temple of the Japanese Buddhist Order in Vienna.

Hang Out Waterside

BARS AND STREET ART

MAP: **1** P70 **A5**

One side of the **Danube Canal** (Donaukanal) is within the 2nd district's borders – and is packed full of bars, buzz and street art. Between the **Augartenbrücke** (Augarten Bridge) and **Franzensbrücke** (Franz' Bridge) is a promenade smattered with restaurants and waterside dens, community gardens, sculptures and expressive murals. The canal became the legalised area for graffiti in the mid-'90s, keeping the Innere Stadt polished. Walk this open-air stretch of urban art covering every space from the walls to the bridge arches. On warmer days, this strip is packed and the hot spot for sundowners. But you don't even have to enter an establishment – bring your own drinks and join the locals sitting along the banks.

THE DANUBE'S SANDY SHORES

There's not a real beach in Vienna, but some of the banks of the Danube's tributaries in the neighbouring 22nd district have been transformed into sandy shores. On the Neue Donau (New Danube), recreational **Copa Beach** (MAP: **2** P70 **H2**; *copabeach.wien*) brims with sand banks and hut bars; the nearest U-Bahn station is Donauinsel (U1). The bougie **Vienna City Beach Club** (MAP: **3** P70 **H2**; *vcbc.at*) complex has deckchairs, a volleyball court, DJ sets and a cocktail bar.

The Alte Donau (Old Danube) has its own island, home to the **Strandbad Gänsehäufel** (MAP: **4** P70 **H2**; *gaensehaeufel.at*) – a self-contained swimming pool complex complete with a beach, restaurants and kayak hire.

Stroll a Baroque Garden with WWII Bunkers

PUBLIC GARDEN

MAP: **5** P70 **A2**

Augarten – the tip of the triangle of parks above Stadtpark and Prater – is often overlooked. If you come here, you'll find yourself in the manicured hedgerow maze of Vienna's oldest baroque garden, though not without its dark history looming. The park is punctuated by two of Vienna's six concrete **Flaktürme** (flak towers) – the above-ground air-raid-defence bunkers from 1944. Fortunately, the Augarten survived destruction. The former imperial hunting ground from 1614 was expanded by Habsburg rulers over the century, with Emperor Joseph II allowing public access in 1775.

Look Inside the Porcelain Palace

FACTORY AND MUSEUM

MAP: **6** P70 **B3**

The palace isn't a residential relic but rather houses the **Augarten Porcelain Manufactory** and

Porzellanmuseum *(Porcelain Museum; augarten.com; museum entrance adult/child €8/free, guided tour €21/free)* – the second-oldest porcelain factory in Europe, which still produces Habsburg classics, the candy-striped Josef Hoffmann collection from 1929, alongside contemporary collaborations including Italian fashion designer Giambattista Valli.

You can trace Vienna's decorative pottery-art history, dating to its inception in 1718, in the small but beautifully presented two-floored museum, or browse the shop for free. You'll need deep pockets for this prized porcelain.

Watch the Vienna Boys' Choir Perform CONCERT HALL

MAP: **7** P70 **G1**

Augarten has quite a musical lineage. Mozart, Schubert and Strauss performed here, and today the acclaimed Vienna Boys' Choir has its concert-hall home, **Das MuTh** *(muth.at),* on the garden's southern tip, with a regular schedule of afternoon and evening performances throughout the year. Ballet, opera and musical productions by young talent are top of the bill.

Traipse Around the Trendsetting District Quarters NEIGHBOURHOODS

Between Hollandstrasse/ Leopoldsgasse and Taborstrasse, and spreading a little outside this street ladder, is the **Karmeliterviertel** (Carmelite Quarter; MAP: **8** P70 **F3**) – the happening subdistrict of Leopoldstadt. Here you'll find boutique and secondhand clothing stores, cool cocktail bars, bohemian vegan, indie-cool and cubby-hole cafes, Italian aperitivo spots and a slew of hip restaurants serving schnitzel.

At the weekend, the humming weekday corner of the **Karmelitermarkt** (Carmelite Market; MAP: **9** P70 **E3**) is a bohemian magnet – come here on Fridays and Saturdays for the farmers market and join the ranks of locals packing out the grid of gastronomy stalls from Vietnamese to vegetarian bites.

Shedding its former sketchy persona through slow gentrification, the **Stuwerviertel** (MAP: **10** P70 **G4**), northeast of Prater, is the latest area of Leopoldstadt gaining ground in its hip hangout offering. **Vorgartenmarkt** (MAP: **11** P70 **G4**)– though overshadowed by Karmelitermarkt   has always been a market mainstay, but the growth of old *Beisl* turned modern pubs, casual bars and hip coffee joints is giving new life to this lesser-known quarter.

See p70 for map of locations

Best Places for...

🄶 Budget 🄶🄶 Midrange 🄶🄶🄶 Top End

Eating

Karmelitermarkt Bites

Cafemima 🄶

 12 E2

Kitsch cafe with outdoor seating, healthy breakfast bowls and homemade lemonades. *8.30am-10pm Tue-Fri, 8am-2pm Sat, 9.30am-5pm Sun*

Ugis Gemüsekebap 🄶

13 E2

This joint specialises in vegetable-loaded, plant-based doner and wraps, generously portioned. *11am-9pm Mon-Fri, 10am-6pm Sat*

Tre Viet 🄶

14 F3

Small Vietnamese bistro serving pho, banh mi and weekly noodle and curry specials. *10am-8.30pm Mon-Fri, 8am-6pm Sat*

Classic & Contemporary Austrian

Skopik & Lohn 🄶🄶

15 E1

This *Beisl* turned trendy bistro in the Karmeliter-viertel is known for one of

the city's best schnitzel. *6pm-midnight Tue-Sun*

Das Loft 🄶🄶🄶

16 B6

Breakfast, fine dine or sip cocktails at this spectacular rooftop restaurant-bar. Panoramic skyline views look towards Stephansdom and Prater. *6.30-10.30am & 6-10pm Mon-Fri, 7am-noon & 6-10pm Sat & Sun*

Sperling im Augarten 🄶🄶

17 B3

Serene palace-set restaurant serving modern Austrian fare and a seasonal menu, with a terrace overlooking the park. *9am-10pm Tue-Sat, to 6pm Sun*

Schöne Perle 🄶🄶

 18 E2

Modern joint with *Beisl* nostalgia, serving tradi-tional regional fare, vege-tarian and fish mains, and Austrian wines. *11am-11pm Mon-Fri, 10am-midnight Sat & Sun*

Brösl 🄶🄶

 19 G4

This former *Beisl* was given a modern pub revival and today dishes

up a daily-changing menu of seasonal, organic fare and beverages. *5-11pm Mon-Thu, to midnight Fri & Sat*

Luftburg Kolarik im Prater 🄶🄶

20 G6

The world's largest fully certified organic restau-rant is set in an urban garden within the amuse-ment park. *4-11pm Mon & Tue, from 11am-Wed-Sun*

Vegan

Harvest Café-Bistrot 🄶🄶

21 B5

The district's bohemian vegan bedrock is an inviting vintage living room. Kebab, variations on Viennese classics, salads and mezze. *2-10pm Mon-Sat, from 10am Sun*

Italian

Pizza Mari' 🄶

22 E1

The tastiest Neapolitan pizza this side of the canal, best enjoyed with an aperitivo or spritz. Pizza serving hours vary. *noon-midnight Tue-Sat, to 11pm Sun*

Monte Ofelio
 F1

Neapolitan hangout on the edge of Augarten with cheese and antipasti plates, strong drinks and a lively atmosphere. *5-10pm Tue-Fri, from 10am Sat*

Drinking

Coffee

ihana
 E1

Finnish cubby-hole cafe in the Karmeliterviertel serving Nordic coffee, *Smørrebrød* (butter bread) snacks and cinnamon buns. *8.30am-5pm Tue-Fri, 9am-3pm Sat, 11am-3pm Sun*

Balthasar
 C6

Praterstrasse's contemporary coffee bar serves artisanal brews from sustainable coffee roasters, plus wine and champagne. *7.30am-7pm Mon-Fri, 9am-5pm Sat*

Laid-Back Bars

Central Garden
 D6

Canalside hole-in-the-wall bar and cultural hub, with garden deck and indoor seating, perfect for beer, wine and light bites. *4-11.30pm Mon-Sat, 2-10pm Sun*

Hafenkneipe
 D6

Open-air waterside bar with rustic seating and a relaxed community vibe. You'll usually find stickleback fish and pizza vendors serving, too. *5-11pm Mon-Sat, 4-10pm Sun*

Brendl
 F3

In a deep-red, chandeliered room, cosy Brendl is a trendy place to linger over coffee or a drink. *5pm-1am Sun-Thu, to 2am Fri & Sat*

MADAI aperitivobeisl
 F3

This retro-decorated bar-bistro blends Austrian and Italian flavours. It's an aperitivo and spritz hot spot. *11am-midnight Tue-Thu, to 1am Fri & Sat*

Cocktails

Bar Pigalle
 B6

Casual-cool bolthole near Nestroyplatz offering classic cocktails and creative specials. *6pm-1.30am Tue-Thu, to 3am Fri & Sat*

Hammond
 G2

The district's long-standing classic cocktail bar: warm wood interiors, plush seating and award-winning mixologists. *6pm-1am Mon-Thu, to 3am Fri & Sat*

fritz von stuwer
 H4

This cocktail bar in the Stuwerviertel is akin to a living room fitted out with vintage furniture. A great playlist to boot. *5pm-midnight Mon-Sat*

Shopping

Vintage & Streetwear

Shop around the Corner
 E2

Small but quality retro store stocking vintage and designer secondhand clothing and accessories handpicked by the owner. *1-6pm Tue-Fri, to 5pm Sat*

Montana Store Vienna
 G2

Street art enthusiasts will find more than just spray cans here, with a selection of books, streetwear and art prints. *11am-7pm Mon-Fri, 10am-6pm Sat*

See p95 for eating, drinking and shopping listings

Explore
Belvedere & Beyond: Landstrasse

Landstrasse exudes a quiet elegance in its boulevards, parks and landmarks, with the splashy 18th-century baroque palace and UNESCO World Heritage Site, Schloss Belvedere, as its centrepiece. Once the stately home of Prince Eugene of Savoy, Belvedere is today an art museum of masterpieces, including *Der Kuss* by Gustav Klimt. The heart of the 3rd district can be found between here and the canal: in the city's Stadtpark and the Hauptstrasse and Ungargasse lined with opulent architecture leading to it. In its residential corner is a second art collection but of a different kind, the Hundertwasserhaus, transformed to be untypical with modern architectural styles which harmonise with nature.

Getting Around

 Walk

It takes around 30 minutes to walk from the Belvedere Museums to the Hundertwasserhaus, taking in the architectural avenues along the way.

U-Bahn (Metro)

Südtiroler Platz (U1) is closest to Schloss Belvedere, Landstrasse (U3, U4) to the Hundertwasser House. Use Schlachthausgasse U-Bahn (U3) for Marx Halle, and Erdberg (U3) for the Arena music venue.

 Tram

From Stubentor, opposite Stadtpark, tram line 1 gets you to the Hundertwasser House in 10 minutes, and Tram D heads south to Schloss Belvedere in less than 15.

Johann Strauss statue, Stadtpark (p93)
ANNE RICHARD/SHUTTERSTOCK

THE BEST

MONUMENT & GALLERY
Schloss Belvedere (p86)

GREEN ESCAPE
Stadtpark (p93)

UNIQUE ARCHITECTURE
Hundertwasserhaus (p93)

MUSEUM
KunstHausWien Museum Hundertwasser (p94)

BEACH BAR
Strandbar Herrmann (p93)

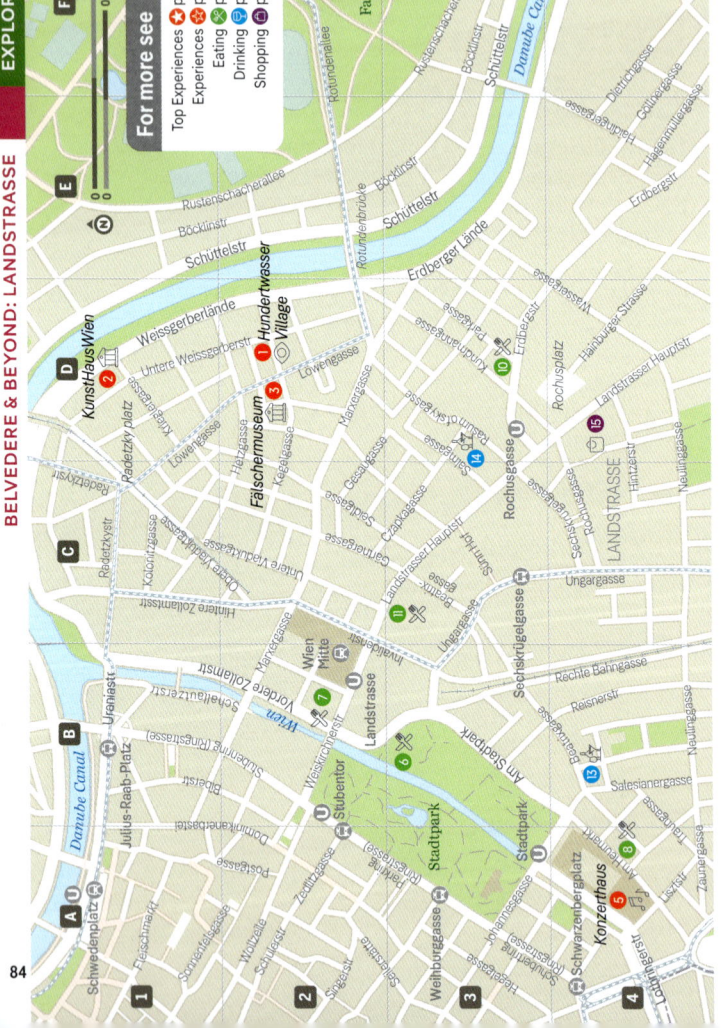

For more see

Top Experiences		p86
Experiences		p94
Eating		p95
Drinking		p95
Shopping		p95

KunstHausWien

Hundertwasser Village

Fälschermuseum

Konzerthaus

Stadtpark

Wien Mitte

Danube Canal

Unterer Prater Fasangarten

LANDSTRASSE

500 m
0.25 miles

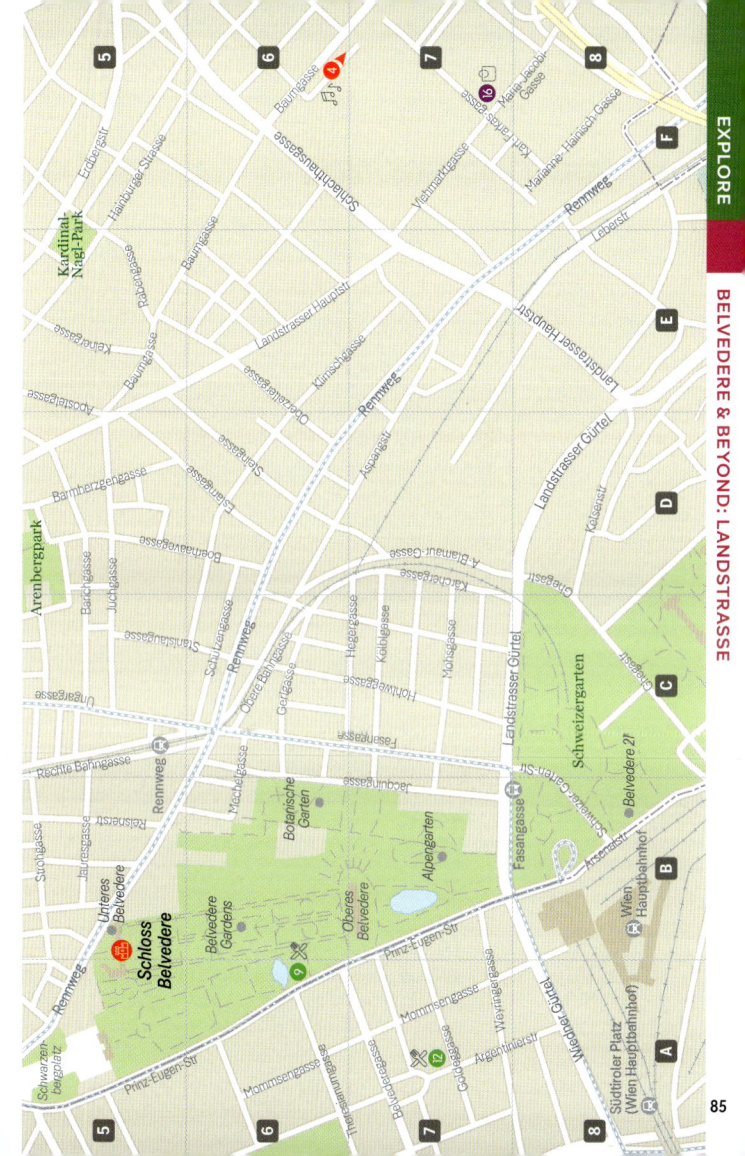

★ TOP EXPERIENCE

Schloss Belvedere

Prince Eugene of Savoy's exquisite baroque Schloss Belvedere from 1723 is a masterpiece. A legacy assemblage of art and architecture three centuries on, the dual complex is a trove of Austrian art from the Middle Ages to the present day and displays the world's largest collection of Klimt works.

MAP P84 **B5**

PLANNING TIP
You'll need at least half a day to visit the art collections and the grounds. All gardens, except the Kammergarten (Privy Garden) and Alpengarten (Alpine Garden), are free to enter.

Scan this QR code to purchase discounted timed entry tickets.

Oberes Belvedere: The Permanent Collection

As an esteemed military general to the Habsburgs, Prince Eugene of Savoy's construction of Belvedere was nothing short of a show of power, commissioning famous baroque architect Johann Lukas von Hildebrandt to design this overtly opulent summer residence. The prince was also an art connoisseur who filled it with his worldly collections, which Empress Maria Theresia later turned into the Imperial Picture Gallery in 1777, opening one of Vienna's first public museums.

Rising splendidly above the gardens, the **Oberes Belvedere** (Upper Belvedere; *adult/child €21/free*) presents a dizzying display of grandeur. From the white vaulted **Sala Terrena**, ascend the Grand Staircase with its stucco reliefs to reach the gilded, ochre-coloured **Marble Hall**. Prince Eugene brought Italian fresco artists Carlone, Chiarini and Fanti to Vienna to paint the ceilings. That famous view of the city? It's from the balcony right here.

The halls may be ordered by an 800-year chronological timeline of styles, but they go beyond a display of artisanship. With mood-changing, multi-hued halls, it presents the collection in the context of the era it was made, spotlighting the

JOHANNES STOLL/BELVEDERE, VIENNA

social, political and cultural periods and events that shaped the artist and their work, including war and migration, ideal environments and subjective inner worlds.

The halls left of the Marble Hall house the extravagant **Austrian Baroque** (1600–1800), alongside harmonious **Neoclassicism**, imaginative **Romanticism** and highlights of realism-based **Viennese Biedermeier** (1880–65). A highlight is Franz Xaver Messerschmidt's *Character Heads* depicting human emotions in portrait busts.

The seven halls to its right house the revered **Vienna 1900** collection. It's an expressive display of progression from avant-garde artists of the Klimt-led Viennese Secession, such as Koloman Moser, alongside their international Impressionist contemporaries like Monet, Renoir and Van Gogh and Expressionist successors, including Munch and Schiele. It all climaxes

HISTORIC VENUE
Upper Belvedere's Marble Hall was the location for the milestone signing of the Austrian State Treaty in 1955 between the Allied powers, re-establishing Austria's independence.

QUICK BREAK
Beyond the classics, enjoy an English breakfast, panini or vegetarian curry in the Art Nouveau salon of the 1910 Viennese coffee house **Café Goldegg** (p95) on the fringes of the palace grounds.

with Gustav Klimt's most famous work, *Der Kuss* (The Kiss), which, of his 22 paintings here, never leaves the gallery. If you're beelining for this, it's at the very end of the wing close to the octagonal preserved Palace Chapel.

The 2nd floor continues the development of the art journey through **Emerging Modernism (1900–20)** and postwar, boundary-pushing **Avant-Gardes (1920–50)**. On the ground floor, there's the dynamic **Avant-Gardes of the 1960s & 1970s**. Despite the dash to the Marble Hall, chronologically, the collection begins down here with the **Middle Ages to the Renaissance (1200–1600)**; the frescoed Carlone Hall entrance is an astonishing sight.

JOHANNES STOLL/BELVEDERE, VIENNA

Unteres Belvedere: The Home of Prince Eugene

Temporary exhibitions continue the story of the Moderne Galerie (Modern Gallery) established in **Unteres Belvedere** (Lower Belvedere; *adult/child €18/free*) in 1903, but, really, this is the ticket to enter Prince Eugene's illustrious world. Built between 1712 and 1716, Lower Belvedere was his extravagant residential wing.

Another **Marmorsaal** (Marbled Hall) entrance dazzles, but look back for the prime view of Upper Belvedere, before moving on to the fanciful floor-to-ceiling painting display in the **Groteskensaal** (Hall of Grotesques) and the white stuccoed **Marmorgalerie** (Marble Gallery) built to display figurine sculptures. The gilt and porcelain-plated, mirrored **Goldkabinett** (Gold Cabinet) is the gaudy showstopper, a refurnished design stamp of Maria Theresia that has been displayed in its original condition since 1765.

The **Orangerie** (Orangery) conservatory turned modern temporary exhibition space connects to the Austrian medieval artwork-filled **Prunkstall** (Palace Stables) and the tranquil **Kammergarten** (Privy Garden), hidden from the view of the public palace gardens.

Belvedere Gardens: Stroll in Baroque Beauty

Belvedere means 'beautiful view', an expression realised most from the **Belvedere Gardens** (pictured left). Both visitors and locals come here to freely stroll the three-terrace baroque greenery set between the twin Belvederes; Parisian-born Prince Eugene is said to have been inspired by the Palace of Versailles, and it shows.

The entrance to Upper Belvedere on its south side features the **Grosse Bassin** (large basin), a pond intentionally designed to reflect the image of the palace. Temporary exhibitions often incorporate artworks on the water. It takes around 10 minutes to walk through the symmetrical

BEST ARTWORKS OF OBERES BELVEDERE

Klimt's *Der Kuss* (The Kiss) is a standout, but following are some of the best of the vast collection of 24,000 works:

• *Napoleon at the Great St Bernhard* (Jaques Louis David; 1801)

• *Self-portrait as a Young Man* (Ferdinand Georg Waldmüller; 1828)

• *The Cook* (Claude Monet; 1882)

• *The Plain of Auvers* (Vincent van Gogh; 1890)

• *Judith* (Gustav Klimt; 1901)

• *Dreams* (Helene Funke; 1913)

• *The Family* (Egon Schiele; 1918)

• *Self-Portrait with a Comb* (Marie-Louise von Motesiczky; 1926)

• *224 The Big Way* (Friedensreich Hundertwasser; 1955)

Schloss Belvedere & Gardens

Prunkstall
(Royal Stables)

**Schloss
Belvedere**

Orangery

Kammergarten

Unteres Belvedere
(Lower Belvedere)

Rennweg

Ungargasse

*Lower
Cascade*

Belvedere
Gardens

Mechelgasse

Prinz-Eugen-Str

Muschelbrunnen

*Upper
Cascade*

Stöckl
im Park

Botanischer
Garten

Oberes Belvedere
(Upper Belvedere)

Belvederegasse

Jacquingasse

Fasangasse

*Grosse
Bassin*

Alpengarten

Weyringergasse

Landstrasser Gürtel

Wiedner Gürtel

Arsenalstr

Schweizer-Garten-Str

Schweizergarten

Wien
Hauptbahnhof

Belvedere
21

Südtiroler Platz
(Wien Hauptbahnhof)

N

0   400 m
0   0.2 miles

parterres and guarding Sphinx statues from the five-stepped **Upper Cascade** and ornamental **Muschelbrunnen** (Shell Fountain) to the **Lower Cascade** trickling Vienna's spring water. The seated nooks within the topiary rows closer to Lower Belvedere are atmospheric hidden corners.

Tucked behind the trimmed hedgerows are neighbouring gardens. The Upper Belvedere's **Botanischer Garten** (Botanical Garden; *admission free*) was added by Maria Theresia in 1754. Today it cultivates 11,000 plant species from six continents and is a space for scientific research. The **Alpengarten** *(adult/child €4.50/€3.50),* established in 1865, is one of the oldest alpine gardens in Europe, nurturing some 4000 species including roses, rhododendron and a display of 100 Japanese bonsai.

Belvedere 21: Contemporary Art Space

Belvedere's contemporary experimental and interactive art space is a fantastical space to find yourself in. The red, steel-glass Modernist box structure – formerly the Museum of the 20th Century, or the 21er Haus – was designed by Austrian architect Karl Schwanzer and initially constructed for the Austrian Pavilion for the 1958 World Exhibition in Brussels. It was revived as **Belvedere 21** *(belvedere21.at; adult/child €11/ free)* in 2011, displaying a changing rota of 20th- and 21st-century art and film screenings.

Its encompassing sculpture gardens, including the permanent display of cuboid stack designs and the iconic giant pink baseball cap by Austrian sculptor Fritz Wotruba, are free to access.

Belvedere 21 is a 10-minute walk south of the palace complex in the **Schweizergarten**.

BUZZING DISTRICT
Empress Maria Theresia founded the first beekeeping school in Augarten in 1769; today some two million are abuzz in the city. Of the 456 species, 130 of them call the Botanical Garden of the University of Vienna in the Belvedere Garden home. Neighbouring Hotel Daniel and the KunstHausWien (p94) join the slew of hotels and museums in hosting the mighty buzzers.

WALKING TOUR

Landstrasse's Green Escapes

Catch some fresh air outside the art-filled galleries on this walk through Vienna's 3rd district. From flak towers reclaimed by parkland to a chromatic apartment block sprouting a rooftop forest, a buzzing beach on the Danube Canal and repurposed military grounds, you'll see how the city has been reshaped by nature.

START	END	LENGTH
Arenbergpark	Schweizergarten	6km; 1½hr

1 Nature Reclaims

One block east from the Landstrasse Hauptstrasse is **Arenbergpark** whose large trees enclose the peaceful urban park and reclaim the space taken by two wartime *Flaktürme* (flak towers). The park's origins date back to 1785, when a garden was constructed for the Esterházy Palace that once stood here.

2 Market Corner

Compact **Rochusmarkt** has everything from butchers to *Blumen* (flowers), its many floral stalls continuing the trade from when it was exclusively a flower market. If you're feeling peckish, there's a handful of cheese and fresh produce stands as well as cafes and taste-laden establishments like Arrigo Bar and El Gaucho Steakhouse.

3 Urban Eco-Living

Eccentric artist Friedensreich Hundertwasser's design ethos was to create spaces where human beings and nature can coexist harmoniously. Deliberately visually deviant from its conventionally classical neighbours with its motley paintwork, curvy lines and forest-sprouting balconies and rooftop, the **Hundertwasserhaus** achieves its goal of getting people to stop and think about city planning and ecological living.

4 Canalside Beach

The 3rd district is home to the inner-city's only beach, **Strandbar Herrmann** (*strandbarherrmann. at*). Grab a deckchair and umbrella, order a spritzer and some street food bites, feel the sand under your feet and see the Donaukanal as your ocean. Come here also for DJ sets, beach yoga and silent beach discos.

5 City-Centre Hideaway

On the district's northern fringes is the **Stadtpark** – Vienna's first municipal park, opened in 1862. While typically considered a 1st district darling with its golden statue of Johann Strauss, half of it falls within Landstrasse's boundaries – a promenaded, woodland link between the city and the inner district. The park is spliced by the Wien River (Wienfluss), whose staircase bridge Wienflussportal (Vienna River Portal) offers a scenic viewpoint.

6 Military History Repurposed

Southernly **Schweizergarten** (Swiss Garden) occupies a space in front of the imposing red-brick former military arsenal constructed after the revolution against imperial troops in 1848, part of which tells Vienna's war-torn history in the **Heeresgeschichtliches Museum** (*Museum of Military History; hgm. at*). The old training grounds were remodelled into an English garden in 1904 when the city expanded; today it's a sculpture-dotted green space and history walk.

Peek at Eco-Living Design

UNIQUE ARCHITECTURE

MAP: **1** P84 **D2**

The famed viewing point of the wacky Hundertwasserhaus (p93) is on Kegelgasse; unfortunately you can't enter this private apartment building. The touristic **Hundertwasser Village** opposite is valuable for a closer glimpse at the bulbous ceramic columns, mosaics and undulating levels that define the artist's signature style.

Another facade view is on **Löwengasse**, with a small shop and indoor cafe playing an aged documentary-style film about the building design – the only chance you'll get to satisfy your curiosity about what's on the inside.

Lose Yourself in Hundertwasser's World

ART MUSEUM

MAP: **2** P84 **D1**

The **KunstHausWien Museum Hundertwasser** (Art House Vienna; kunsthauswien.com; adult/child €16/7), replete with Hundertwasser hallmarks, is a permanent gallery of the artist's paintings, scale models and blueprints of his other structural works in Austria.

The uneven floors create an experience Hundertwasser saw as 'a melody of the feet'; more often than not, they stop you in your tracks to admire more of his work on display. Other gallery space is dedicated to temporary exhibitions on social-environmental topics. There's also a tree-enclosed cafe.

Eye the Art Fakes

ALTERNATIVE ART MUSEUM

MAP: **3** P84 **D2**

You'll need a sharp eye to spot the difference in this one-of-a-kind display of genuine forgeries in the tiny **Fälschermuseum** (Museum of Art Fakes; faelschermuseum.com; adult/child €8.50/free). Displayed next to an image of the original, the museum tells the stories of infamous forgers and how they hoodwinked the experts.

Rock Out at a Former Slaughterhouse

LIVE MUSIC VENUE

MAP: **4** P84 **F6**

A former slaughterhouse site turned music venue, **Arena Wien** is one of the edgier places to catch alternative music acts. Metal, rock, punk and rap acts play the open-air stage in the summer months; in winter, bands play in one of the venue's two indoor halls.

Catch a World Music Performance

CONCERT HALL

MAP: **5** P84 **A4**

The classical music behemoth **Konzerthaus** (konzerthaus.at) presents its seasonal catalogue of 750 performances – including jazz, pop and world music – across four simultaneously staging halls. Vienna Hofburg Orchestra concerts (unless held at the Hofburg) take place in the Mozart-Saal (Mozart Hall).

Guided tours (adult/child €8.50/€4) in English take place at 2pm Friday.

Best Places for...

G Budget **GG** Midrange **GGG** Top End

See p84 for map of locations

EXPLORE

BELVEDERE & BEYOND: LANDSTRASSE

Eating

High End

Meierei im Stadtpark **GGG**

6 B3

Cafe-restaurant of Austria's top-rated Michelin venue, Steirereck, has bountiful breakfasts and 150 types of cheese. *8am-11pm Mon-Fri, 9am-7pm Sat*

Bistros & Restaurants

Das Suess'kind **GG**

7 B2

Cosy bistro and takeout with an organic, plant-based daily menu. *11am-3pm Mon-Fri*

Gmoakeller **GG**

8 A4

This atmospheric tavern has been plating up classic grub since 1858. *11am-11pm Mon-Sat*

Stöckl im Park **GGG**

9 A6

Atmospheric dining in a garden, serving regional specialities to complement the in-house brewery offering. *11.30am-11.30pm*

Habibi & Hawara **GG**

10 D3

Feast on Middle Eastern flavours at Vienna's first restaurant run by refugees. *11.30am-5.30pm Tue-Fri, 9am-3pm Sat & Sun*

Cafes

Joseph Brot **GG**

11 C3

There's no place better for a wholesome breakfast than at one of the capital's finest bio bakeries. *7.30am-7pm Mon-Fri, to 6pm Sat, to 4pm Sun*

Café Goldegg **GG**

12 A7

Linger in the Art Nouveau–style salon of this 1910 coffee house serving Viennese classics. *8am-8pm Mon-Fri, from 9am Sat & Sun*

Drinking

Rooftop

Caya Coco

13 B4

Cuban-inspired hangout with prime views over the Stadtpark and historic centre. *hours vary*

Alternative

Das Moped

14 D3

Casual-cool industrial-clad and retro-furnished bar with tap beers, Austrian wines, spritzers and cocktails. *5pm-2am Mon-Sat*

Shopping

Artisan

Lingenhel

15 D4

Indulgent deli with fine cheeses, salumi, sweets and select spirits. The bar-restaurant serves Austrian-European fare using seasonal, market-fresh ingredients. *9am-6pm Tue-Fri, to 2pm Sat*

Pop-Up Market

Wild im West

16 F7

This hip pop-up urban bar and lounge hosts a weekend *Flohmarkt* (flea market) and bi-weekly night market, with trendy clothing and vinyl, ending with evening DJ sessions. *3-8pm Sun*

See p108
for eating,
drinking and
shopping
listings

Explore
Naschmarkt & Around: Wieden & Mariahilf

Southwest of the Ringstrasse spills the 4th (Wieden) and 6th (Mariahilf), the downtown inner districts mixing urban grunge with historical grand. They meld with village-like compactness but remain distinguishable by the anchor Naschmarkt and are characterised by narrow streets, street art, creative stores, multicultural cafes, restaurants and trendy bars. At Wieden's core is architectural Karlsplatz, a lively garden-flanked square where seasonal festivities are staged in front of its baroque church, Karlskirche. In Mariahilf, the Naschmarkt, a bustling open-air food paradise and Vienna's most famous market, is a whirl of street-food vendors rubbing shoulders with cool dining options.

Getting Around

 Walk

Once here, the districts are easily connected on foot; it takes around 10 minutes to walk between them, with Naschmarkt wedged in between.

U-Bahn (Metro)

Reach the 6th district's Gumpendorfer Strasse from the MuseumsQuartier (U2). South of it lies the 4th district, accessible by Kettenbrückengasse (U4) at Naschmarkt's western end and Karlsplatz (U1, U2, and U4) on its eastern tip, closest to the Freihausviertel.

Tram

The Ringstrasse tram lines 1, 2, D and 71 stop at Oper/Karlsplatz.

Flohmarkt am Naschmarkt (p107)

MARIA MASLOVA/SHUTTERSTOCK

★

THE BEST

HISTORIC MONUMENT
Karlskirche (p101)

MUSEUM
Wien Museum (p100)

UNIQUE EXPERIENCE
Sewer Tour (p103)

FOOD & DRINK
Naschmarkt (p107)

ARCHITECTURE
Otto Wagner Pavillon (p103)

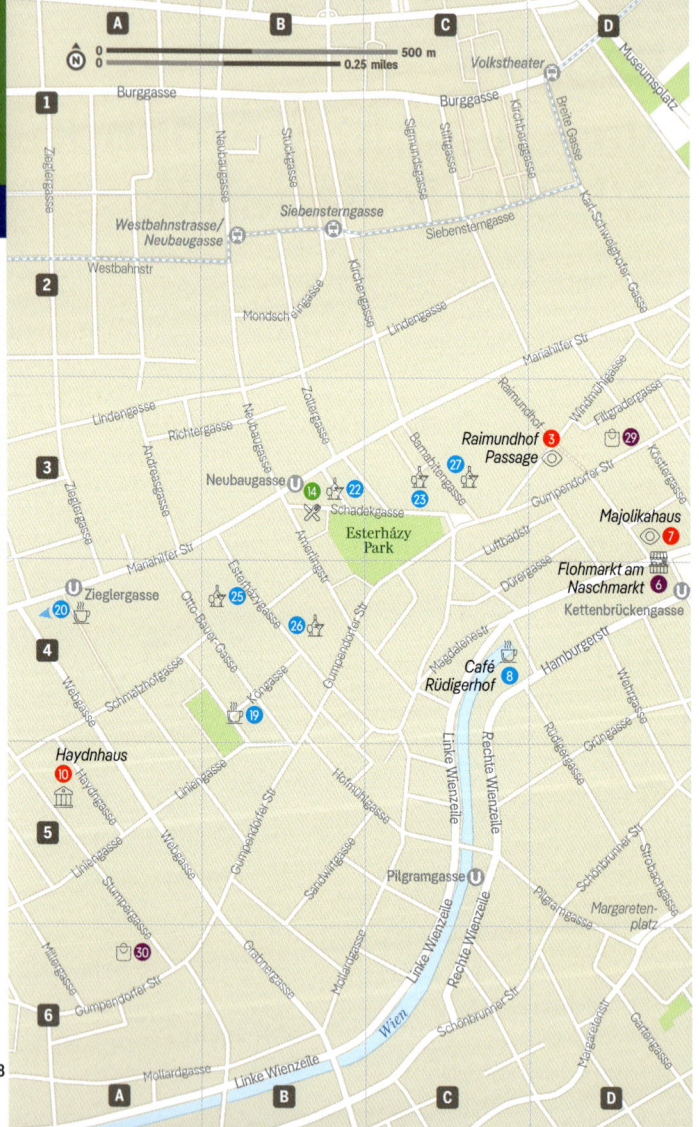

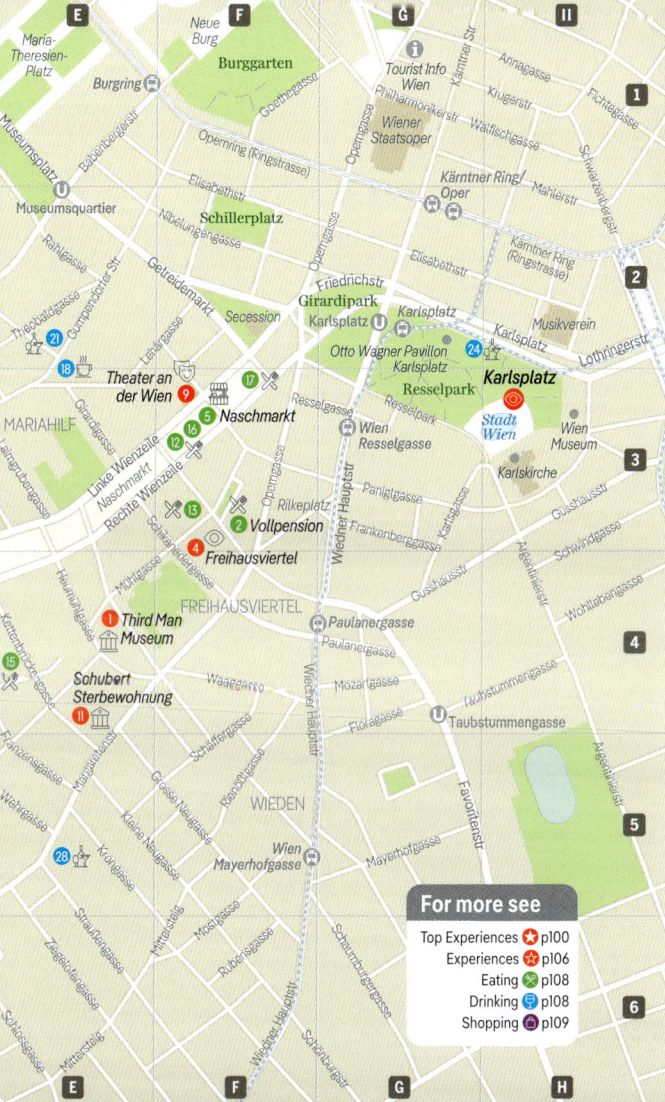

E
Maria-Theresien-Platz
Neue Burg
F
Burgring
Burggarten
G
Tourist Info Wien
Wiener Staatsoper
Philharmonikerstr
Annagasse
Krugerstr
Kärntner Str
Fichtegasse
1

Opernring (Ringstrasse)
Goethegasse
Operngasse
Walfischgasse

Babenbergerstr
Elisabethstr
Museumsplatz
Museumsquartier
Schillerplatz
Nibelungengasse

Kärntner Ring / Oper
Mahlerstr
Kärntner Ring (Ringstrasse)
2

Rahlgasse
Getreidemarkt
Friedrichstr
Girardipark
Karlsplatz
Secession
Karlsplatz
Elisabethstr
Musikverein
Karlsplatz
Lothringerstr

Theobaldgasse
Gumpendorfer Str
21
18
Theater an der Wien
9
Naschmarkt
17
5
Landesg
Otto Wagner Pavillon Karlsplatz
24
Karlsplatz
Resselpark
Resselgasse
Stadt Wien
Wien Museum
Wien Resselgasse
3

MARIAHILF
16
12
Linke Wienzeile
Naschmarkt
Rechte Wienzeile
Operngasse
Resselgasse
Paniglgasse
Karlskirche
Gusshausstr

Laimgrubeng
Köstlergasse
13
Rilkeplatz
2 Vollpension
Wiedner Hauptstr
Frankenberggasse
Gusshausstr
Schwindgasse
Argentinierstr

Schleifmühlg
4
Freihausviertel
Müllerg
Schleifmühlgasse
FREIHAUSVIERTEL
1 Third Man Museum
Paulanergasse
Paulanergasse
Wohllebengasse
4

Heumühlg
15
Schubert Sterbewohnung
11
Waaggasse
Mozartgasse
Floragasse
Taubstummengasse
Favoritenstr
5

Kettenbrückeng
Margaretenstr
Schäffergasse
Gleich Neugasse
Wiedner Hauptstr
Taubstummengasse
Argentinierstr

Fendigasse
Kleine Neugasse
WIEDEN
Wien Mayerhofgasse
Mayerhofgasse

Wehrgasse
Schönbrunner Str
28
Kleine Neugasse
Kleine Neugasse
Mittersteig
Mostgasse
Schaumburgergasse
Schönburgstr
Favoritenstr
6

Schlossgasse
Ziegelofengasse
Rubensgasse
Wiedner Hauptstr

For more see		
Top Experiences	⭐	p100
Experiences	✴️	p106
Eating	✖️	p108
Drinking	☕	p108
Shopping	🛍️	p109

E **F** **G** **H**

Karlsplatz

Karlsplatz has a long history of urban transformation: from medieval wall glacis terrain to the architectural grounds for the post-plague Baroque Karlskirche, a Ringstrasse-era school (now part of the Technical University), Otto Wagner's Stadtbahn and the modern 1950s Wien Museum building.

MAP P98 **H3**

PLANNING TIP
Plan ahead. The Wien Museum is closed on Monday; the Otto Wagner Pavillon is only open Friday to Sunday; and the seasonal sewer experience runs just one English tour per day.

Scan this QR code for the Wien Museum's special exhibition listings.

Charting Urban History

The remodelled **Wien Museum** *(wienmuseum.at/wien_museum; permanent exhibition free)* chronicles the history of Vienna across three floors, featuring an ensemble of 1700 objects and scaled models intricately detailing its evolution.

The **ground floor** starts with the Palaeolithic-era and moves forward in time from there, featuring a mammoth tusk, a Roman stone relief (pictured) from the eastern gate of the Vindobona fortress and medieval sculptures from St Stephen's Cathedral among its displays.

The art, attire and architecture showcase on the **1st floor** spans the period from 1700 to 1900, timelining the rise of the empire, the aftermath of the Napoleonic Wars and the Industrial Age.

The 'Since 1900' exhibit on the **2nd floor** charts Vienna's acceleration to becoming a European cultural centre; displays include Klimt's 1902 portrait of Emilie Flöge and his blue smock, the only surviving garment of the artist. It moves to more provocative social discourse, starting with the Social Democratic 'Red Vienna' cultural achievements after WWI, Austria's annexation into the German Reich in 1938 and Vienna's postwar story.

The **3rd-floor terrace** has an elevated side view of Karlskirche and features a revolving artist showcase on its muralled rooftop. The top **4th floor** is reserved for temporary special subject

LISA RASTL, WIEN MUSEUM

exhibitions *(from €12)*; past topics have included city architects and the Allied Forces in Vienna.

The Baroque Architectural Centrepiece

Karlsplatz is named after Emperor Karl VI, and his commissioned baroque **Karlskirche** (St Charles's Church; *karlskirche.eu; adult/child €9.50/5)* after the plague saint Charles Borromeo. The church was constructed from 1716–37 on the emperor's solemn vow after the 1713 plague. Designed by Schloss Schönbrunn architect Johann Bernhard Fischer von Erlach, it's an architectural pick 'n' mix of Greek temple, Roman arch and Byzantine elements, with a marbled pilaster nave and baroque frescoed interior (ticketed entry).

Climb a level for a closer balcony view of the dome frescoes by Johann Michael Rottmayr, depicting God answering the saint's prayers to end the plague. The panoramic terrace is the closest

QUICK BREAK
In the neighbouring trendy Freihausviertel, fuel up on classic grub like pork schnitzel or hearty pub staples like lasagne at the legendary bohemian *Beisl* **Cafe Anzengruber** (p108).

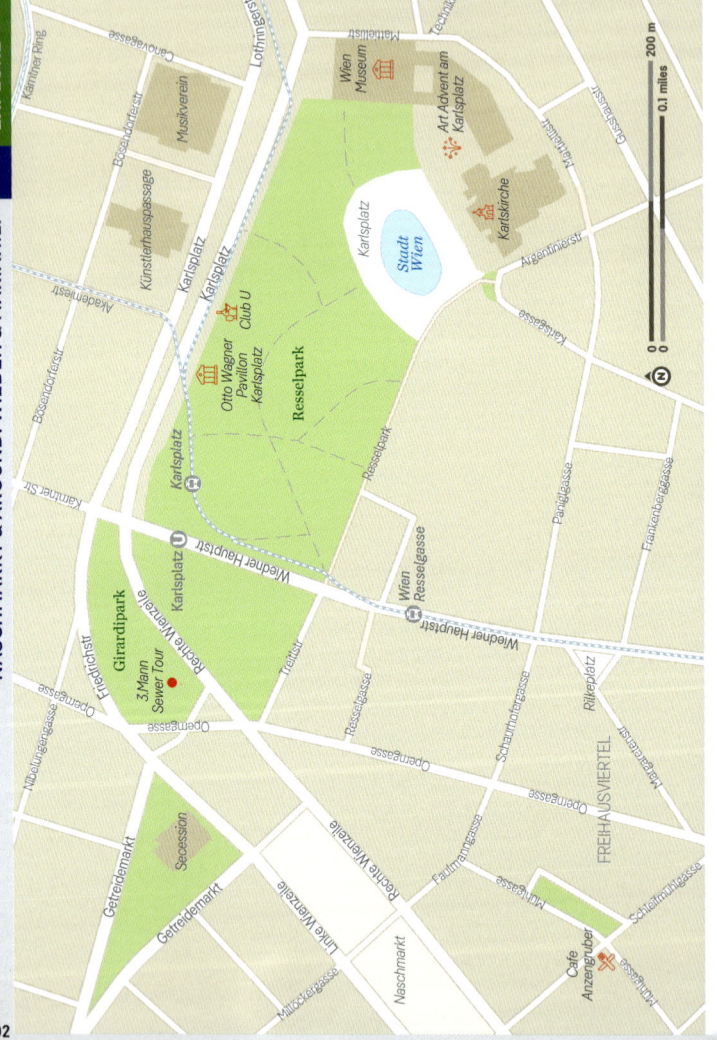

you'll get to the 72m-high dome; it overlooks Karlsplatz with views of Stephansdom's south spire.

Viennese Modernism Monument

Otto Wagner, the pioneer of 20th-century Viennese Modernism, trailblazed Vienna's landscape with his functionalist, high aesthetic designs. A significant project was the construction of the Stadtbahn (Vienna metropolitan railway). The pavilion at Karlsplatz, dating to 1898, served as a station alongside Emperor Franz Joseph's Hofpavillon (Court Pavilion) at Hietzing, while the converted U-Bahn stations Schönbrunn and Stadtpark (U4), Währinger Strasse-Volksoper and Josefstädterstrasse (U6) are some of the best preserved.

The **Otto Wagner Pavillon Karlsplatz** (*wienmuseum.at/otto_wagner_pavillon_karlsplatz; adult/child €5/4*) is a signature green-and-gold-accented exhibition space dedicated to Wagner's life and work. Its twin portal opposite is a converted cafe and home of music **Club U** (p109).

A Subterranean Exploration

Film history was made when postwar Vienna became the setting for the 1949 Orson Welles film noir classic, *The Third Man*. You can retrace the scenes of protagonist Harry Lime from Prater's giant Ferris wheel and in the historic centre on the **Third Man Walking Tour** (*viennawalks.com; €26*).

However, for a radical kind of exploration head to Karlsplatz Girardipark, where you can helmet up and get into an older part of the capital's waste-water system on a guided **3.Mann Sewer Tour** (*drittemann tour.at; adult/child €10/5*). It's actually far from grim; instead, a tunnelled light-projection show along a walkway looks at subterranean Vienna while reliving the famous chase scene. Between May and October, tours run from Thursday to Sunday, with only one English tour daily at 3pm. Spaces fill fast so book well ahead online.

SEASONAL FESTIVITIES
The biggest events on the square are the four-day expressive and experimental music festival Popfest featuring Austrian acts in July and the creative display of the **Art Advent am Karlsplatz** that unfurls in front of the illuminated baroque Karlskirche come November. Shop from handpicked makers of leather, metal, wood, ceramic, glass and visual arts, and stay for the live music.

🚶 **WALKING TOUR**

Shop in Style: Mariahilf to Freihausviertel

From the artisan to the antique, step into style on a shopping trail from Mariahilf to Wieden's Freihausviertel neighbourhood. Flip through vinyl in a movie scene record shop, linger in a book-stacked cafe, bag a brew of the city's best coffee, spice up your kitchen and discover sustainable, upcycled and historical home and fashion wares.

START	END	LENGTH
Teuchtler Alt & Neu	Bananas	1.7km; 25min

① Vinyl Movie Scenes

Film buffs will recognise the interior of the **Teuchtler Alt & Neu** record shop, established in 1948. It was one of the backdrops of Richard Linklater's 1995 film *Before Sunrise,* where American Jesse and French Céline take a romantic romp through Vienna, though the listening booth used by the pair here no longer exists.

② Ethical Home Style

Modish design and sustainability are central to the home concept store **Raumkomplett**; founder Doris Ackerl made it Austria's first shop to label every product with clear social and eco credentials. Books, decor, desk accessories and furniture, all ethically handcrafted in Europe.

③ Bookworm Bolthole

Creative cafe and curated book shop, **Phil** is Vienna's stylish living room on grungy Gumpendorfer Strasse. By day, you'll find locals reading in retro-furnished nooks or conversing over coffee and snacks, while evening switches gears with readings and film screenings.

④ A Viennese Roast

Aromatic **Alt Wien Kaffee** has been roasting organic, fair-trade beans since 2000; founder Christian Schrödlf's mission is to produce the city's best coffee. More than 40 varieties of fresh beans are sold – blends or pure varieties, arabicas and robustas, already packaged, or ground and bagged in front of you. Sip a brew at the little on-site bar.

⑤ Spice Rack Heaven

The flagship store of kitchen haven **Babette's** is an around-the-world culinary wonderland of cookbooks and own-brand spice blends, with regular servings of home-baked treats and spice tastings.

⑥ Upcycled Wears

Upcycling and social responsibility underpin the quirky designs at **Gabarage**, where discarded materials are given a second life. Old tarpaulins are transformed into bags, traffic lights into home lamps, bowling pins become vases, and books are repurposed into stools.

⑦ Glamorous Vintage Wears

FLO Vintage is home to historic designer fashion. From the accentuated styles of the late 1800s and Art Deco elegance of the 1920s to experimental '60s and the statement glam of the '70s and '80s, this place is a trove of high-quality, collectable pieces.

⑧ Trendy Antique Treasures

An antique store with retro flair, **Bananas** brims with bar trolleys, writing tables, upholstered chairs, lamps and trinkets. Come here to browse for one-of-a-kind furniture, ornamentation and jewellery objects from the 1930s–1970s.

EXPERIENCES

Continue the Third Man Trail

MUSEUM

MAP: **1** P98 **E4**

Take a cinematic deep dive 10 minutes on foot from the sewer tour location. Thousands of items from film props, photos, scripts and documents are exhibited in the district's **Third Man Museum** (*Dritte Mann Museum; 3mpc.net; adult/child €12/8),* privately run by

NAVIGATE THE CREATIVE QUARTER

MAP: **4** P98 **F3**

There are no definitive boundaries of the **Freihausviertel**, but navigate the grid lanes between Faulmanngasse-Paniglgasse and Pressgasse, and you'll find yourself in the thick of this creative cluster of stores and stomping grounds. Rechte Wienzeile below Naschmarkt is the highway of East Asian restaurants and supermarkets; Schaurhofergasse houses a Japanese supermarket and teahouse. Schleifmühlgasse brings together everything retro and cool with its cafes, vintage and hip stores. Kettenbrückengasse and Margaretenstrasse may take you into the 5th district, but their absorption into the Freihausviertel's funkiness, with smash burger joints and trendy wine bars, is seamless.

movie enthusiasts. Download the free audio guide.

Break for a Coffee & Cake with Meaning

CAFE

MAP: **2** P98 **F3**

Vollpension *(Full pension; vollpension.wien)* is the city's only generational cafe concept where you can experience the Austrian *Jause* (break time over food) with the warmth of its Oma and Opa (grandma and grandpa) hosts. Find a space in the vintage-decorated, brick-painted living room, order snacks, drinks and homemade cakes prepared by the city's favourite grandparents, and engage in heartwarming conversation. A meaningful initiative to combat loneliness and poverty in old age, it's a place baked in love and nostalgia.

Wander Along a Historic Alleyway

SHOPPING PASSAGE

MAP: **3** P98 **D3**

Take a trip through the 18th century between Windmühlgasse 20 (north of Naschmarkt) and the shopping strip of Mariahilferstrasse 45. The **Raimundhof Passage**, named after thespian and playwright Ferdinand Raimund since it charts a route through his birth house, is a tucked away cobblestoned connection of staircases and courtyards filled with modish artisan stores and teeny cafes. The Secret Garden's inner courtyard hideaway is a retreat from the high street.

Indulge the Senses   FOOD MARKET

With bursts of colour, tantalising aromas and the bustle of restaurants wedged in between, a walk through the 120 food stalls of **Naschmarkt** (*Naschen* meaning the joy of eating something sweet; MAP: **5** P98 **F3**) offers the chance to sample diverse flavours. Vienna's biggest market started as a fruit and veg seller at Freyung, relocating to its current home and expanding as the Wien Fluss (Wien River) was levelled (it's still there underneath it all). Its trio of pavilion laneways remain largely unchanged since 1902.

The bazaar switches gears on the weekend. On Saturday join bargain hunters and antique hawkers at the **Flohmarkt am Naschmarkt** (MAP: **6** P98 **D4**), sifting through clothing, rummaging through boxes and perusing trinkets to the sounds of energetic price-calling and the hum of haggling.

Admire Modernism in Construction   ARCHITECTURE

On the road parallel to Naschmarkt, you can admire another of Otto Wagner's designs at the decoratively tiled **Majolikahaus** (MAP: **7** P98 **D3**; *Linke Wienzeile 40*), not without the architect's signature gold and green finishes.

The nearby Secessionist building **Rüdigerhof** (*Hamburgerstrasse 20*) with its plaster swirl facade was built in 1902 by Wagner student Oskar Marmorek; get a closer look from its in-house **Café Rüdigerhof** (MAP: **8** P98 **C4**).

Get Tickets to a Revived Historic Stage   THEATRE

MAP: **9** P98 **F3**

Since its opening in 1801, the **Theater an der Wien** (*theater-wien.at; standing room/seat from €9/29*) has been the home of operas, operettas and musicals, hosting monumental premiere performances, including Beethoven's *Fidelio,* Mozart's *The Magic Flute* and Johann Strauss II's *Die Fledermaus.* These days it stages traditional greats alongside contemporary revivals. It reopened in late 2024 after extensive renovations.

One-hour **backstage tours** (*adult/child €9/€6.50*) of the house Mozart's librettist built run up to four times a week from July to May.

Follow the Last Years of a Musical Genius   COMPOSER HOUSES

The last 12 years of Haydn's life were spent in the now 6th district **Haydnhaus** (MAP: **10** P98 **A5**; *wienmuseum.at/haydnhaus; adult/child €5/free*), composing his notable works *The Creation* and *The Seasons.*

Though bereft of personal objects, Schubert enthusiasts can picture where the Vienna-born composer penned his last musical drafts at the 4th district **Schubert Sterbewohnung** (MAP: **11** P98 **E4**; *wienmuseum.at/schubert_sterbewohnung; adult/child €5/free*), the apartment where he died in 1828.

Best Places for...

⊖ Budget **⊖⊖** Midrange **⊖⊖⊖** Top End

See p98 for map of locations

Eating

Austrian

Zur eisernen Zeit **⊖⊖**

 F3

Naschmarkt's oldest *Beisl* has been here since 1916 and cooks one of the city's heartiest *Gulasch* (paprika-spiced meat stew) as well as a tasty *Wiener Schnitzel. 11am-11pm Mon-Sat, to 5pm Sun*

Cafe Anzengruber **⊖⊖**

 F3

This legendary 4th district *Beisl* adds a trendy sheen to tradition, serving classics, including pork schnitzel, alongside modern dishes like stuffed peppers and lasagne. *4pm-1am Tue-Sat*

Motto Brot **⊖**

 B3

Streetside bakery of the chic Parisian-Viennese Art Deco hotel, with organic sourdough loaves and sandwiches and a delectable patisserie spread. *7am-7pm Mon-Fri, from 8am Sat, 8am-5pm Sun*

XO-Grill **⊖⊖**

 E4

Street-food grill joint with a mission to eat meat better – the beef used in its signature smash burgers, pastrami and Philly cheesesteak sandwiches is sourced from retired Austrian dairy cows. *noon-10pm Mon-Sat, to 8pm Sun*

Naschmarkt Picks

Käseland **⊖⊖**

 F3

Naschmarkt's specialist cheese shop is a local favourite, though its European delicacies are best sampled with a platter and wine-tasting session on its cosy outdoor terrace. *9am-6.30pm Mon-Fri, 8am-6pm Sat*

Umarfisch am Naschmarkt **⊖⊖⊖**

17 **F3**

This upscale fish and seafood restaurant has fine tartare, carpaccio and soup starters, and signature mussel and shrimp dishes. *11am-10pm Mon-Sat*

Drinking

Coffee Houses

Café Sperl

18 **E2**

The *Jugendstil*-fitted 1880 coffee house and artist's living room on Gumpendorfer Strasse was where the founders of the Secessionist art movement met. An inspiring space for *Kaffee und Kuchen* (coffee and cake). *7am-10pm Mon-Sat, 10am-8pm Sun*

Café Jelinek

 B4

Forgo the polished graces and linger in the cosiest of old-timer cafes with its faded wallpaper, picture gallery walls, shabby-chic upholstery and wood-burning stove. *9am-10pm*

Hip Cafes

Good Coffee Society

 A4

Sample third-wave brews of European roasters at this hip, cubbyhole hub, stocked with coffee varieties you'll unlikely find anywhere else. *8am-5.30pm Mon-Fri, 9am-6pm Sat, 10am-5pm Sun*

Phil

 E2

Lounge in reading nooks at this cool combo of cafe, bar and curated bookshop on Vienna's grungy Gumpendorfer Strasse. *2-9pm Mon, 9am-10pm Tue-Thu, 9am-11pm Fri & Sat, 9am-9pm Sun*

Alternative Bars

Tanzcafé Jenseits

22 **B3**

This boudoir bar is a very Viennese institution. Kitsch and eccentric, the dimly lit, wallpapered place is a pocket, the dance floor small and the patronage a wild mix. *9pm-4am Wed-Sun*

Futuregarden

23 **C3**

Grungy, art-pasted bar with outdoor terrace opposite the concrete hulk of the Haus des Meeres aquarium. Perfect for a no-thrills beer, wine or spritz. *5pm-2am Mon-Thu, to 4am Fri, 4pm-4am Sat, 7pm-1am Sun*

Club U

24 **G2**

Youthful two-floor bar and club hangout with live bands and DJ sets occupying one of Otto Wagner's Stadtbahn Pavilions on Karlsplatz. The outdoor

seating area overlooks the main pavilion and park. *7pm-4am Wed-Sat*

Cocktail Bars

Barfly's

25 **B4**

Sophisticated speak-easy-type den famous for its extensive cocktail list. An intimate and ambient space located at the back of the Art Deco Die Josefine Hotel, with teal tones, velvet upholstery and gold trims. *6pm-2am Mon-Thu, to 3am Fri & Sat, 7pm-1am Sun*

Miranda Bar

26 **B4**

With a pink pastel feature wall and turquoise marble counter, Miranda is a bright take on Vienna's typical cocktail dens and favoured by a young crowd. Creative variations of classics and adventurous concoctions are served. *6pm-midnight Mon-Wed, to 1am Thu-Sat*

Craft Beer & Wine

Ammutsøn Craft Beer Dive

27 **C3**

Craft beer bar on a cobbled alley with communal bench seating and quirky art on its white-brick walls. Twelve taps pour independent brews from Austrian and European craft breweries. *4pm-2am Mon-Thu, to*

4am Fri, 2pm-4am Sat, 2pm-midnight Sun

Pub Klemo Weinbar

28 **E5**

Wine bar with pub-like atmosphere in the 5th district offering up to 100 wines by the glass, from Austrian to rare and fine varieties. Homemade pasta and antipasti dishes are the perfect accompaniment. *5pm-midnight Mon-Sat*

Shopping

Naturally Viennese

Saint Charles Apotheke

29 **D3**

The emporium of the Viennese herbal remedy brand is not only an interior spectacle in ornate carved dark wood, but also stocks some 300 hair, skin and medicinal products. Its cosmetics outpost is opposite. *8am-6pm Mon-Fri, to 1pm Sat*

Augora Fermente

30 **A6**

Dedicated entirely to the craft of wild fermentation, the on-site store of the restaurant has a stock of their homemade and naturally organic foods and seasonings. *10.30am-7pm Tue-Fri, to 5pm Sat*

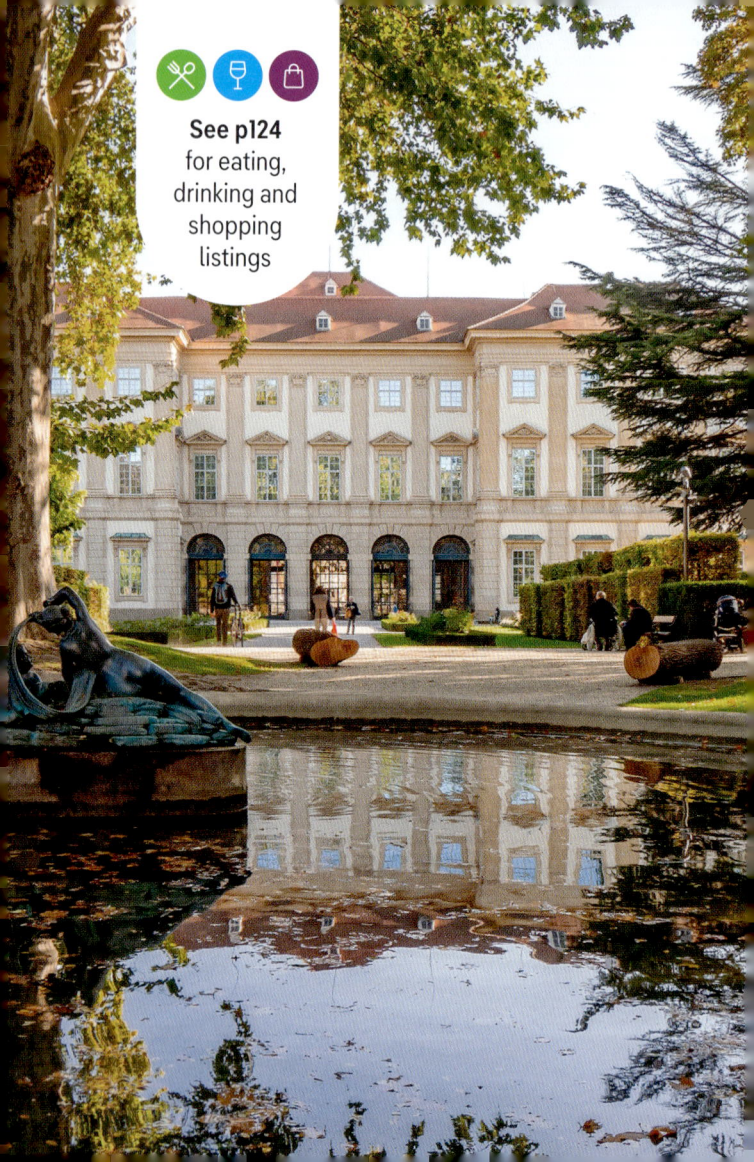

See p124 for eating, drinking and shopping listings

Explore
Neubau, Josefstadt & Alsergrund

Bordering the Ringstrasse to the west are the inner districts of the 7th (Neubau), 8th (Josefstadt) and 9th (Alsergrund). Start at the MuseumsQuartier (MQ) art and culture complex, Neubau's creative nucleus, from which unfolds an upmarket hip hub of concept stores, fashion boutiques and high-end drinking and dining. The bourgeois 8th residential pocket makes for a charming architectural add on as you move towards the bon vivant 9th, where you'll find Sigmund Freud's flat and the baroque Gartenpalais Liechtenstein, thriving creative corners in the haute-culture hamlet of Servitenviertel, and the gritty waterside Spittelau and its Hundertwasser-designed waste incinerator.

Getting Around

 Walk

It's a 10-minute walk from the Hofburg to Neubau's MuseumsQuartier, Spittelberg and Burgasse.

U-Bahn (metro)

For Neubau (7th), Volkstheater (U3) and MuseumsQuartier (U2). Josefstadt (8th) spills behind Rathaus (U2) onto the central thoroughfare, Josefstädter Strasse. Alsergrund (9th) sites are within a 10-minute walk from Rossauer Lände (U4).

 Bus

The 13A bus runs from Alser Strasse in the 8th district to and from the Hauptbahnhof (main train station), passing through the 7th and Naschmarkt. Tram line D goes to the 9th.

Gartenpalais Liechtenstein (p121)
MISTERVLAD/SHUTERSTOCK

THE BEST

CULTURAL SPACE
MuseumsQuartier (p114)

MUSEUM
Sigmund Freud
Museum (p122)

SHOPPING
Neubaugasse (p120)

PALACE
Gartenpalais
Liechtenstein (p122)

UNUSUAL SITE
Spittelau Incinerator (p122)

111

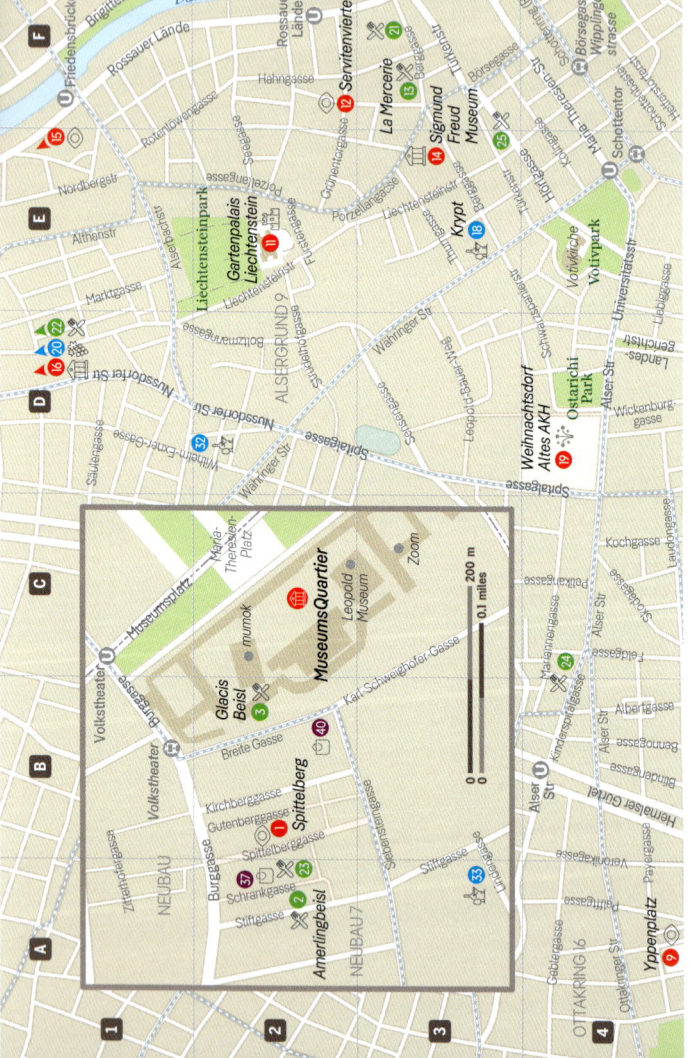

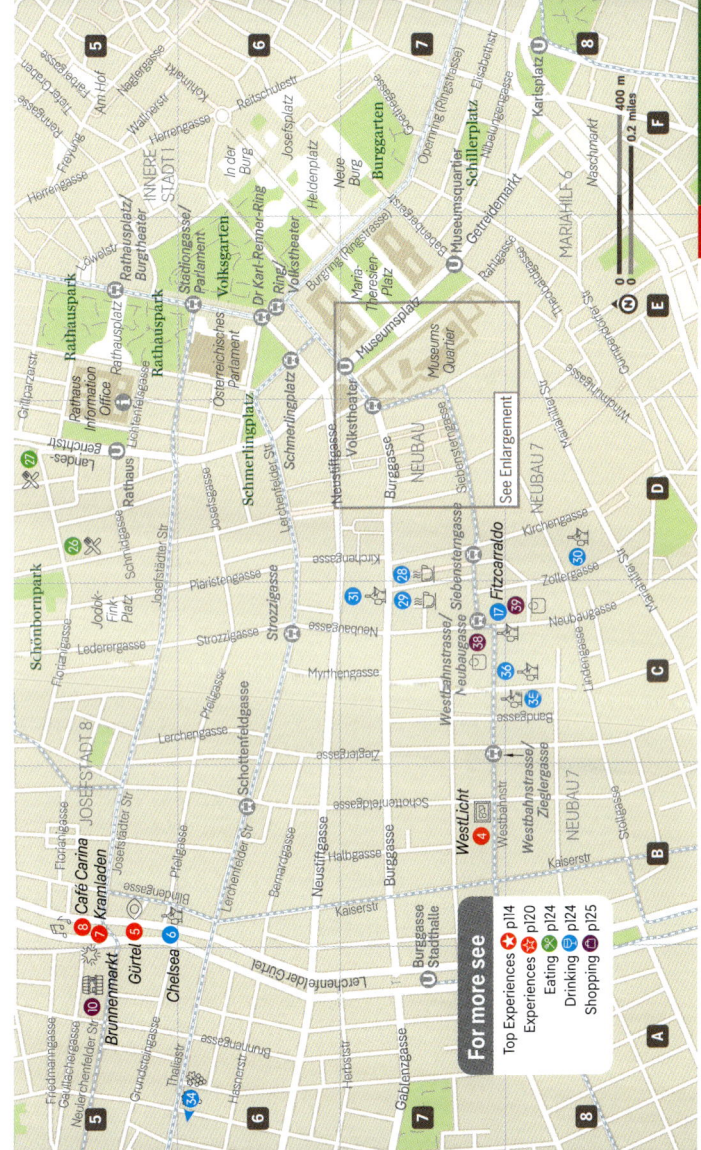

For more see

Top Experiences ⭐ p114
Experiences ● p120
Eating ✕ p124
Drinking 🍷 p124
Shopping 🛍 p125

★ **TOP EXPERIENCE**

MuseumsQuartier

The MuseumsQuartier (MQ) occupies the former baroque court stables, once part of the imperial assembly of structures that included Maria-Theresien-Platz galleries and the Hofburg. A revival of an historical heirloom, it has become one of the world's largest cultural districts with its arsenal of 11 exhibition spaces. The visually competing eggshell-white cube (Leopold) and grey basalt hull (mumok) are the star attractions.

MAP P112 **C2**

PLANNING TIP
The courtyard is open 24/7. Museum entry times vary: mumok and Kunsthalle Wien are closed on Monday; Leopold Museum on Tuesday. On-site bars close between 10pm and midnight.

Scan this QR code for current exhibitions and combined ticket options.

Leopold Museum

If Belvedere was an introduction to Modernist art, **Leopold** (*leopoldmuseum.org; adult/child €17/2.50*) is your graduation. More than 8300 works across five exhibition floors compile one of the most important collections of Austrian art of early Modernism; its pride and joy 'Vienna 1900' package covers three.

Moving through Leopold's brightly lit marble interior is an awakening, much like Modernist art was an innovation. Between the world's most comprehensive Egon Schiele collection (which includes 44 paintings and over 200 watercolours, drawings, prints and texts), Gustav Klimt's 1910 masterwork *Death and Life* and exhibits detailing the Viennese Secession movement and *Jugendstil* (Art Nouveau) design, you get to understand the birth of Modernism and its sociopolitical context.

Leave time for a stop at rooftop **MQ Libelle** (*admission free*) – the glass-fronted terrace here has views overlooking the museum complex towards the Hofburg.

mumok

A journey through **mumok** (Museum of Modern Art, Ludwig Foundation Vienna; *mumok.at; adult/child €18/free;* pictured right) and its 13,000-piece collection of 20th and 21st century art is meant to

CRISTI CROITORU/SHUTTERSTOCK

shock and stir your senses, ignite discourse and challenge perceptions. Its a galaxy of contemporary works transition from sparky exhibits to the darkened nexus bathed in natural light.

Move from Expressionist Classical Modernism; experimental pop and conceptual art of the 1960s and 1970s avant-gardes; the radical expose of the taboo and tragic in 20th-century Vienna Actionism to the provocative Contemporary evolution. The museum's film and photography works expand the collection.

The Modern Trio with More Time

If you plan to hang around longer in the converted stable halls, three other exhibitions fill out the five-strong art offering.

Vienna might be a European epicentre for creativity, but two exhibitions hand over the floor to international artists. The small, passage wing-set **MQ Freiraum** hosts contemporary

QUICK BREAK
Rest and refuel without leaving the complex with organic plates at **MQ Kantine**, takeout bites and beverages from **MQDaily**, Italian cuisine at **Halle** and Southeast Asian fare at **Café Leopold** on the top floor of Leopold Museum.

YEAR-ROUND EVENTS

The courtyard hosts a winter and summer programme, from open-air performances to DJ nights and the Winter at MQ Christmas market with light projections.

material art and installation displays, while the larger **Kunsthalle Wien** (*kunsthallewien.at; adult/child €12/free*) showcases pieces from places typically overshadowed by dominant European art capitals. Programmes run between three to six months and focus primarily on sociopolitical themes, bolstered by multimedia installations. Baroque remnants from the former Winter Riding Hall are incorporated into the exhibition infrastructure on its ground floor. Admission is free every Thursday from 5pm to 9pm.

If you've wandered Vienna and noticed a layered design, the permanent exhibit 'Hot Questions – Cold Storage' at the **Architekturzentrum** (Architecture Centre; *azw.at; adult/child €12/9;* pictured) unravels it. The industrial-clad hall features sketches, scale models, videos and images of Vienna's urban

ARCHITEKTURZENTRUM (ARCHITECTURE CENTRE) VIENNA

planning and Austrian architecture of the 20th and 21st centuries, from the revolutionary to the unrealised. A second hall hosts special shows on international architectural practices and transformations.

Public Micro Museums & Show Rooms

MQ's public baroque art passages tunnel you through worlds of imagination before you've even hit the courtyard. Sound art echoes in the **Tonspurpassage**; world fonts are scripted in the **Typopassage**; a visual reading room of baroque books awaits in the **Literaturpassage**; a comic display in **Kabinettpassage**; and starry light phenomena in the **Sternenpassage**.

The front-of-house corridors host the **Schau Räume** – a free-to-roam ribbon of artist studios and offices interspersed with installations, getting you closer to resident creativity as it happens.

For a backstage pass and an in-depth look into the world's largest cultural district, join the one-hour **Secret MQ tour** (*mqw.at; adult/child €8/7*). English tours take place at 3pm Saturday.

Children's World of Art

Arts, crafts, animation and themed exhibition stages abound at the MuseumsQuartier's Children's Museum, **Zoom** (*kindermuseum.at; adult/child from €6.50/free*). The sea-themed Ocean playground for toddlers has a ship play deck, while older kids can scribble, sketch and paint in the creative studio workshops, or produce art from objects and game stations in the interactive section. Kids aged eight to 14 can create a masterpiece in the animated film studio; the resulting work is archived in Zoom's digital collection.

Dschungel Wien (*dschungelwien.at; tickets from €13*) is MQ's young artist stage covering a diverse repertoire of musical and puppet theatre, dance and drama performances, with 50 productions across its three stages per season. There are up to three performances daily, mostly in German but occasionally in English.

MQ COURTYARD
People don't visit MQ only for its exhibition halls. As symbolic as the art behind the walls, the furniture of the **MQ courtyard** creates its own canvas. The bold, geometric Enzi chairs were designed to entice people to lounge all day, in all seasons – with good weather, you'll rarely see the MQ Courtyard empty.

WALKING TOUR

Architecture Trail: Neubau to Alsergrund

Wander from Burgasse in the 7th to Berggasse in the 9th, through the three inner districts' most beautiful streets and architectural corners. On a journey between Vienna's smallest house and Freud's abode, find a cobblestoned hamlet, hidden residential courtyards, imperial hospitals, noble palaces and the city's second-highest church.

START	END	LENGTH
Vienna's smallest house	Votivkirche	5.4km; 1¼hr

① The Smallest House & the Old Hamlet

At Burggasse 3, you'll find the **smallest house in Vienna**, a two-storey, 14-sq-metre sliver built in 1872. Today it's the Schmollgruber goldsmith. Off Burggasse, the historical laneways around Spittelberggasse are remnants of the outer city settlement of **Spittelberg**, dating back to 1584.

② Hidden Arcades

At Siebensterngasse 46, walk through the **Adlerhof**, a beautiful arcade from 1874, crossing its five mesmerising courtyards. Later, enter the historic **Freiwilliger Durchgang** (voluntary passage) at Neustiftgasse 16 – a 19th-century bypass created when people opened their courtyards to connect parallel streets.

③ 8th District Architectural Trio

Vienna's oldest theatre in operation, **Theater in der Josefstadt** was opened by Beethoven in 1788. Nearby Jodok-Fink-Platz is dominated by the mammoth baroque **Maria Treu Kirche**, whose foundation stone was laid by Emperor Leopold I in 1698. **Palais Schönborn** is the 1706 work of Johann Bernhard Fischer von Erlach, of Karlskirche and Schönbrunn Palace fame; it houses the Austrian Folk Museum.

④ Imperial Hospital History

The lively **Campus der Universität Wien** is still called by its former name, Altes AKH (Altes Allgemeines Krankenhaus; Old General Hospital), a part of Emperor Joseph II's societal reforms, which included this mega hospital of 1784. Look for **Narrenturm** (Fool's Tower), a five-storey cell complex used for mentally ill patients; it's now the Pathological-Anatomical Museum.

⑤ Noble Legacy

On Strudlhofgasse, walk 11 stepped meters down the Art Nouveau staircase, **Strudlhofstiege**. The original 1690 structure on this spot belonged to baroque sculptor and imperial court painter Peter Strudel. Around the corner is the Gartenpalais Liechtenstein (p122), one of the city's two palaces belonging to the Liechtenstein family.

⑥ At Home with Freud

The French-feel Servitenviertel neighbourhood connects to Berggasse. The house at number 19 was Sigmund Freud's family home and workplace for 47 years before having to flee in 1938. Step inside for the **Sigmund Freud Museum** (p122).

⑦ Vienna's Second-Highest Church

The nearby neo-Gothic masterpiece of **Votivkirche** is on the fringes of the 1st district old town. The second-highest church after Stephansdom, it was built as a symbol of gratitude after the failed assassination attempt on Emperor Franz Joseph.

EXPERIENCES

Amble Old Hamlet Alleys   HISTORIC AREA

On a four-lane stretch behind MuseumsQuartier, wander a narrow alley system that has preserved some of the original baroque builds of the suburb of **Spittelberg** (MAP: ❶ P112 **B2**), which sat outside Vienna's city walls. Settlement here dates to 1584, but by 1720 it was a district of 120 houses; the structures not replaced centuries later by classicist and historic buildings still bear date plaques from that time.

The time-honoured laneways of Spittelberg Stiftgasse, Schrankgasse and Gutenberggasse are not just structural heirlooms, however; the area is a thriving creative hub full of stores, studios and dining establishments. For an Austrian meal, try atmospheric **Amerlingbeisl** (MAP: ❷ P112 **A2**), set in a 1700 house with a vine-draped courtyard. It serves sandwiches, seasonal ravioli and chicken schnitzel alongside classic staples. Between MuseumsQuartier and Spittelberg, **Glacis Beisl** (MAP: ❸ P112 **B2**) serves mod-classic Viennese cuisine and Austrian beer and wine, and has garden seating.

The winter **Weihnachtsmarkt am Spittelberg** dials up the charm with over 100 festive booths selling handpicked quality craft woodwork, textiles and metalwares, alongside vegan and organic food.

See Urban Art Beyond the Galleries   STREET ART

The **Calle Libre** (*callelibre.at*) festival has played a part in transforming the urban landscape of Vienna – many of the expressive building murals are a result of inviting local and international artists to come and paint the walls of a different district every August. There are limited English tours or you can download a free map online.

Between Naschmarkt and Burgasse, you'll catch a considerable cluster of colourful works, including *The Mother* monochrome mural covering a house firewall in **Gutenbergpark**, the classical figure on **Siebensterngasse 15**

 AVENUES OF DESIGN

Running from MuseumsQuartier and above the Spittelberg village is one of the oldest streets in Neubau, **Burggasse**, so named for being a parallel highway to the Hofburg. On the stretch to the cross-section of Neubaugasse, the road is a braid of cafes interspersed with design outlets. Come here to sit and people watch. **Neubaugasse**, meanwhile, is almost entirely crammed with artisan design and concept fashion stores and vintage boltholes.

adorning a strip of a building under a modern rooftop, a bird mural covering the side of a classic house at **Karl-Farkas-Park** and the **WestLicht courtyard** extinct species masterwork. Decades ago the Danube Canal became the legalised area for graffiti, keeping the Innere Stadt polished.

Learn About Photography Through the Ages
MUSEUM

MAP: **4** P112 **B7**

The Neubaugasse loft of a former 1950s glass factory now houses the photography gallery and museum **Westlicht** *(westlicht.com; adult/child €12/5)*. It hosts temporary topical photography exhibitions alongside its permanent display of over 360 camera models, arranged in a chronological timeline detailing photography's evolution towards the digital age.

Spend a Night on the Belt Road
ENTERTAINMENT AREA

The peaceful 8th revs up a gear on its district edges. Along the **Gürtel** (belt; MAP: **5** P112 **B5**) road is a near 800m strip of bars and clubs built within the metro rail arches, pumping until the early hours. A cluster of live-music venues around the Josefstädter Strasse U-Bahn station is the alternative epicentre. Long-established musical boozers include the concert and DJ venue **Chelsea** (MAP: **6** P112 **B5**), known for its club nights that rave until 4am; the intimate stage space of **Kramladen** (MAP: **7** P112 **B5**), home

to the English stand-up comedy community; and the grungy **Café Carina** (MAP: **8** P112 **B5**), where you can catch the sessions of home-grown musical talent.

Taste Multicultural Ottakring
MARKET

Across the Gürtel, neighbouring the 8th district, residential **Ottakring** (the 16th) has its spirited soul in the store-and-gallery-hugged and pavilion-filled **Yppenplatz** (Yppen Sq; MAP: **9** P112 **A4**) – the kernel where everything happens. Its daily **Brunnenmarkt** (MAP: **10** P112 **A5**) is Vienna's biggest and most boisterous street market with 170 stalls, busy at weekends when more people gather to find bargains. The nearly 1km of vendor displays on Brunnengasse are a spark of colour and a trailing incense of spices and vegetable stacks, flower bundles and cheese barrels, fresh meats and cooked eats. This multicultural flair and walk through of the world has granted it the nickname 'Orient around the corner'.

Tour the Liechtenstein Home
PALACE

MAP: **11** P112 **E2**

The ruling family of the Principality of Liechtenstein were descendants of Austrian aristocracy, simultaneously residing here with two palaces in the city; the Stadtpalais (city palace; guided tours only in German), which has been renovated to historical glory, in the

THE LITTLE PARIS OF VIENNA
The set-stone street of Serviten-
gasse is the vein of the **Servitenviertel** (Serviten quarter; MAP: 12
P112 **F2**), a thread of lanes surround-
ing the Servitenkirche (Serviten
church). It's known for its high
concentration of speciality cuisine
outlets and indie-owned stores
on its 350m, two-block stretch.
Quaint buildings and fancy French-
style lamppost-dotted, tree-lined
avenues have also given it the
nickname 'Little Paris'. La Mercerie
(MAP: 13 P112 **F3**), the gorgeous
French cafe-bakery here, occupies
a former traditional pharmacy.

Innere Stadt and the **Gartenpalais Liechtenstein** (palaisliechten
stein.com; tours per person €24)
summer residence in the 9th, built
between 1691 and 1711. The latter is
a three-storey ornate work of art,
typically admired from the outside.
Monuments – including the
Golden Chariot in the Sala Terrena,
the frescoes of Vienna's largest
baroque hall, the Herkulessaal
(Hercules Hall), and the 100,000-
book marble library – can only be
seen on one-hour guided visits.
English tours are limited but audio
guides are available on German
tours. The gardens are open and
free to enter, granting a closer look
at this landmark.

Enter Sigmund Freud's Home

MUSEUM

MAP: 14 P112 **E3**

Berggasse 19 is the famous address
of the father of psychoanalysis.
This was Sigmund Freud's family
home and workplace for 47 years
before having to flee from persecution due to the Nazi annexation
in 1938. The **Sigmund Freud
Museum** (freud-museum.at; adult/
child €15/free) provides a look into
the apartment rooms and practice
spaces of the neurologist and his
therapist-teacher daughter, Anna
Freud. The original entrance hall-
way and waiting-room area remain
relatively untouched, allowing you
to step into the home as visitors in
treatment once did.

The remainder of the presenta-
tion is through monochrome-
designed displays that give a
window into Freud as a father
and the development of his life's
work through letters, published
manuscripts, photos, furniture
and private objects, including his
signature spectacles. These rooms
have not been re-created to their
original styling; exhibits and panels are sparsely placed. Almost all
of Freud's methods were developed
and written up here, but don't ex-
pect to see the famous couch – that
was taken into exile in London.

See Where Waste Becomes Art

INCINERATOR

MAP: 15 P112 **E1**

There aren't many places where you
travel to view a waste incineration

plant. Beyond the artist's residential project in Landstrasse, environmentalist Hundertwasser was commissioned to turn the rebuilt heat-production plant in Spittelau into a work of art. He adorned the **Spittelau Incinerator** with his signature kaleidoscopic, checkered facade, added tree-planted terraces and topped the blue-panelled chimney with a gold sphere. Free guided tours take you through the facility and onto its rooftop; see *events.xres.at*. This alternative city skyline landmark stands outside the U-Bahn station and complements the street-art-covered canal arches beneath it.

Waltz Through the Strauss Legacy
EXHIBITION

MAP: **16** P112 **D1**

'Waltz King' Johann Strauss II made the *Blue Danube Waltz* and the dance genre a global icon. While immortalised in gold in Stadtpark, his legacy lives on at the **House of Strauss** (*houseofstrauss. at; adult/child €23/9.50, Strauss concerts from €65*) exhibition, a multi-dimensional delve into the dynasty in the historic Casino Zögernitz, where all four Strauss musicians once played.

Sip Cocktails at a Hidden Bar
COCKTAIL BAR

Hidden behind an inconspicuous vending machine on Neubaugasse, the floral-clad **Fitzcarraldo** speakeasy (MAP: **17** P112 **C7**; *fitzcarraldo-bar. com*) awaits with signature cocktails and plush booth seating

in an Art Deco setting. Meanwhile there's no door sign for the craft-cocktail bar **Krypt** (MAP: **18** P112 **E3**; *krypt.bar*) at Wasagasse 17 – a mysterious entrance to an old cellar turned stylish speakeasy.

Visit a Campus Christmas
CHRISTMAS MARKET

MAP: **19** P112 **D4**

The Altes **Weihnachtsdorf Altes AKH** (Christmas village) at the University Campus courtyard is packed with artwork cribs and chromatic woodland illuminations, curling rinks and lively après-ski style huts. Alpine-esque stands represent each of the Austrian states, offering regional food and drink specialities.

CITY VINEYARDS
MAP: **20** P112 **D1**

Vienna is hedged by 700 hectares of **vineyards**, making it the only European capital to grow significant amounts of wine within its city limits. Head to the fringes and sample an *Achterl* (⅛ litre) of the year's harvest at a rustic *Heuriger* (wine tavern). Since 80% of what's cultivated is of the white-grape variety, start with the famed Grüner Veltliner and Riesling. Red tipplers should try the Zweigelt. Hop on tram line 38 and enjoy urban viniculture in the 19th district village of Grinzing bordering the 9th – **Heuriger Maly**, with its garden courtyard, is a beautiful place to start.

Best Places for...

🅒 Budget   🅒🅒 Midrange   🅒🅒🅒 Top End

See p112 for map of locations

Eating

Austrian

Zum Roten Bären 🅒🅒
21 F3

Bohemian meets quintessential Viennese charm here, where national classics alongside a rotating regional-focused evening menu are served. *5pm-midnight Mon-Fri, from 11am Sat & Sun*

Würstelstand LEO 🅒🅒
22 D1

Vienna's oldest sausage stand and generational institution has been running since 1928. It serves a half-kilo 'Big Mama' *Käsekrainer* if you are ravenous. *10.30am-4.30am Mon-Thu, to 5.30am Fri & Sat, noon-midnight Sun*

Tian Bistro am Spittelberg 🅒🅒
23 A2

The more affordable offspring of Michelin-starred vegetarian restaurant Tian serves sensational regional, seasonal vegetarian and vegan small plates. It has a plant-draped streetside terrace. *5-11pm Tue-Sat*

International

Fratelli Valentino 🅒🅒
24 C4

Pugliese brothers Gianni and Pasquale run a mozzarella (and more) *fromagerie* and bar by day, which turns lively wine and spritz joint by evening. *4-10pm Tue-Thu, from 9pm Fri & Sat*

Der Wiener Deewan 🅒
25 E3

From veggie dhal to meat karahi, this all-you-can-eat Pakistani buffet in a community-driven restaurant is pay as you wish. *11am-11pm Mon-Sat*

Sipsong 🅒🅒
26 D5

The flamboyant restaurant-bar offshoot of legendary Thai eatery Mamamon has its own signature bites and drinks, including special-brewed Sato. *5.30-11.30pm Tue-Thu, to midnight Fri & Sat*

Long Hall 🅒🅒
27 D5

Former beer tavern turned stylish Irish gastropub, with Kozel beer from the tank, bottomless brunch and sports viewing. *11am-1am Mon-Thu, to 2am Fri, 10am-2am Sat, 10am-1am Sun*

Drinking

Cool Cafes & Pubs

Adlerhof
28 D7

A historic building revived with a timeless ensemble of traditional Thonet chairs, teal hues, Art Deco trims and a plant-filled staircase atrium. Choose from breakfast specials, coffee and cake, or an international evening menu. *8am-midnight*

Café Espresso
29 C7

This retro cafe with red-leather banquettes is a hip spot for an espresso, organic breakfast or a glass of natural wine.

7.30am-midnight Mon-Wed, to 1am Thu & Fri, 9am-1am Sat

Café Europa
 D8

Casual, chromatic den that's a longstanding 7th district fixture. Whether for breakfast or a low-key evening, it's a chilled place at all hours. *9am-2am Sun-Wed, to 5am Thu-Sat*

Alternative Pubs
Atlas
 C7

An old *Beisl* transformed into an art gallery and trendy bar-bistro with regional, seasonal fare, speciality coffee, natural wines and craft beers. *4pm-1am Mon-Thu, to 2am Fri & Sat*

Café Clash
 D2

Poster-plastered *Beisl*-bar with tap beers under €5 and a weekly music programme that attracts the cool 9th district dwellers. *6pm-2am*

Wine
R&Bar (Rundbar)
 A3

An Art Deco–inspired wine bar serving only natural options by the glass, alongside a menu of main plates. *4pm-midnight Mon-Fri, 2-11pm Sat*

10er Marie
 A6

Sip local varieties like Grüner Veltliner and Riesling in the neighbouring 16th district at this garden-set tavern. It's the oldest *Heuriger* (wine tavern) in Vienna, dating back to 1740. *3-11pm Tue-Sat*

Creative Cocktail Bars
Die Parfümerie
 C8

Small but swank, this unpretentious cocktail bar has an innovative menu and is a favourite of the Neubau crowd. *6pm-1am Tue-Thu, to 2am Fri & Sat*

Plus43
 C8

You'll need to call to reserve a space and get the coveted door code for entry to this chic hideaway where bartenders whip up tailored concoctions. *8pm-2am Fri & Sat*

🛍 Shopping

Concept Stores
Die Sellerie
 A2

Founded by two graphic designers, this wood-panelled store is filled with European-made, limited-batch homewares, artwork and stationery. *11am-7pm Thu & Fri, to 5pm Sat*

Kitsch Bitch Sight Store
 C7

Forward-looking boutique promoting trendy, emerging Austrian labels including clothing, accessories, jewellery, homeware and trinkets. *11am-7pm Mon-Fri, 10am-6pm Sat*

Park
 C8

Austria's first concept store, opened in 2004 – a bright boutique cube and global design selection of clothing, footwear, accessories and fragrances. *10am-7pm Tue-Fri, to 6pm Sat*

Die Werkbank
 B2

'The Workbench' design collective platforms Viennese designers and their crafts, from sketches and textiles, ceramics and cosmetics. *2-6.30pm Wed-Fri, 1-5pm Sat*

See p137
for eating,
drinking and
shopping
listings

Explore
Schloss Schönbrunn: Hietzing

Known as the noble district, Hietzing (13th district) is half covered by the forest meadows of the former imperial hunting ground, Lainzer Tiergarten, on one side and cradled by the Habsburg summer hideaway of Schloss Schönbrunn on the other. The residential wedge in between is an enclave of the middle-upper class in belts of historic villas filling the once-imperial court domain of nobles and officials. Cornering Schloss Schönbrunn Park is Hietzing's centre, a pocket-sized taste of the enduring stately character beyond the sumptuous as you venture from a classy old imperial guesthouse to classic Viennese culinary institutions.

Getting Around

 Walk
Exit Schönbrunn Gardens via the Hietzinger Tor path; it's a five-minute walk to Hietzing's centre.

 **U-Bahn (Metro)**
Schönbrunn (U4) for Schloss Schönbrunn; Hietzing (U4) for the district centre; Unter Sankt Veit (U4) for the Klimt Villa.

 **Tram & Bus**
Tram lines 10 or 60 from Westbahnhof go to Schloss Schönbrunn. For Lainzer Tiergarten and Hermesvilla, take the 56A and B buses outside the Hietzing U-Bahn station and get off at Lainzer Tor.

THE BEST

HERITAGE SITE
Schloss Schönbrunn (p130)

ARCHITECTURE
Hofpavillon (p136)

PARK
Lainzer Tiergarten (p136)

EXHIBIT
Klimt Villa (p136)

FOR KIDS
Tiergarten
Schönbrunn (p134)

Schloss Schönbrunn (p130)
CANADASTOCK/SHUTTERSTOCK

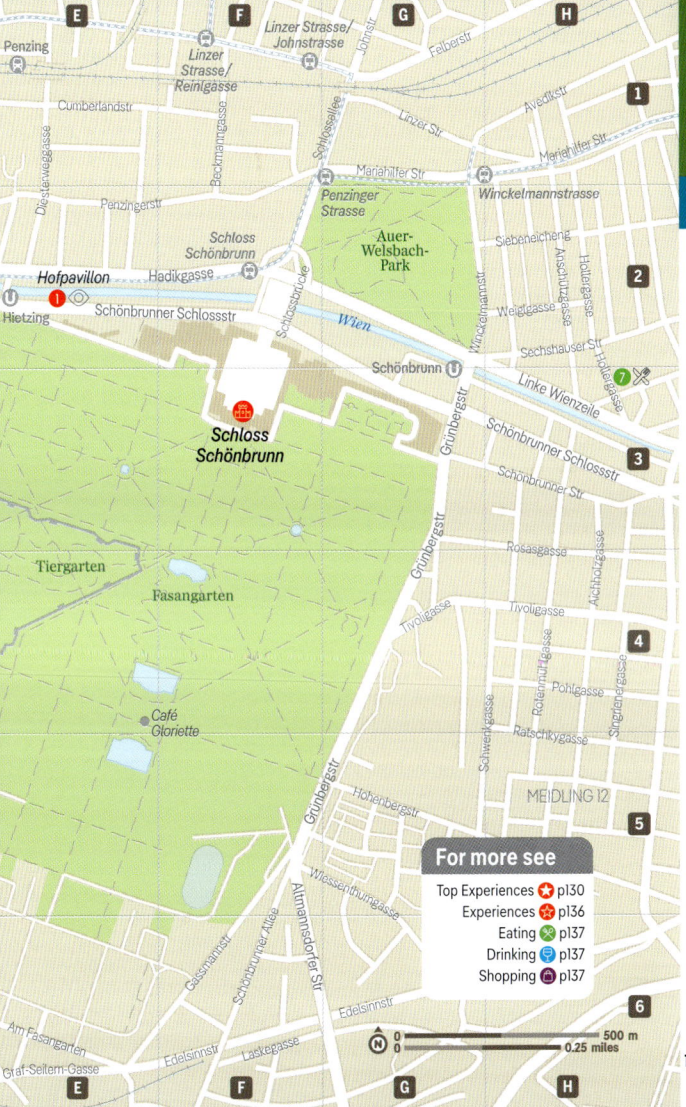

E F Linzer Strasse/ G H
Johnstrasse

Penzing

Linzer
Strasse/
Reinlgasse

1

Cumberlandstr

Avedikstr

Beckmanngasse

Schlossallee

Linzer Str

Mariahilfer Str

Meriahilfer Str

Dieterweggasse

Penzingerstr

Penzinger
Strasse

Winckelmannstrasse

Schloss
Schönbrunn

Auer-
Welsbach-
Park

Siebeneicheng

Winckelmannstr

Anschützgasse

Holtergasse

2

Hofpavillon ❶ 👁

Hadikgasse

Schönbrunner Schlossstr

Schlossbrücke

Wien

Weiglgasse

Hietzing

Sechshauser Str

Schönbrunn Ⓤ

Linke Wienzeile ❼ 🍴

Holzgasse

3

**Schloss
Schönbrunn**

Schönbrunner Schlossstr

Grünbergstr

Schönbrunner Str

Rosasgasse

Aichholzgasse

Tiergarten

Fasangarten

Tivoligasse

Tivoligasse

4

Rotenmühlgasse

Pohlgasse

Singrienergasse

Schwenkgasse

*Café
Gl5riette*

Grünbergstr

Ratschkygasse

MEIDLING 12

5

Hohenbergstr

Wiessenthungasse

For more see

Top Experiences ⭐	p130
Experiences ✴	p136
Eating ✖	p137
Drinking 🍷	p137
Shopping 🛍	p137

Schönbrunner Allee

Cassmannstr

Almannsdorfer Str

Edelsinnstr

6

Am Fasangarten

Edelsinnstr

Laskegasse

Edelsinnstr

🧭 Ⓝ 0 ————— 500 m
0 ————— 0.25 miles

Graf-Seltern-Gasse

E F G H

★ **TOP EXPERIENCE**

Schloss Schönbrunn

No site in Vienna is more entrenched in imperial legacy than Schönbrunn Palace. The city's most iconic Habsburg residence packs a four-century-long timeline of history into its rococo state rooms, ceremonial halls, private apartments and opulent gardens. A saunter through this stately residence is unmissable.

MAP P128 **F3**

PLANNING TIP
The all-in-one ensemble is so remarkable in size you'll want to give yourself at least half a day to experience its majestic heritage.

Scan this QR code for ticket options and to prebook admission.

Schönbrunn History

The site that came into the Habsburg fold back in 1569 grew over centuries into a layer cake of palatial personal stamping. First was the 1642 Château de Plaisance (pleasure palace) of Emperor Ferdinand II's wife, Eleonore von Gonzaga, then the imperial hunting lodge that Emperor Leopold had baroque architect Johann Bernhard Fischer von Erlach build for his son, Crown Prince Joseph. Much of the resplendent overhaul was the work of palace matriarch Empress Maria Theresia during her reign from 1740–80. The grandiose gardens were her last extravagant touch. Schönbrunn remained the favoured Habsburg summer abode, the pinnacle of court life and centre of diplomacy, and in its final years, the home of Empress Elisabeth and Emperor Franz Joseph, who died here in 1916.

Step Inside the Palace

Schönbrunn's size is arresting. There's an exhaustive array of 1441 rooms, of which 40 are open so that visitors can inspect the tastes of the times, with the aid of an audio guide. Rooms 1–18 are a walk through the private living quarters of Emperor Franz Joseph and Empress Elisabeth, including **Franz Joseph's Study** (4), plainly furnished and bedecked in family photographs, the **Empress' Dressing Room** (8) outfitted for a daily

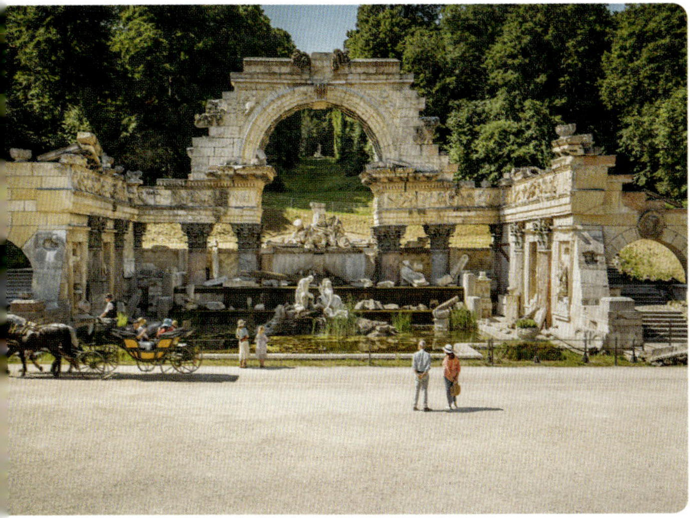

© SCHLOSS_SCHOENBRUNN_KULTUR-_UND_BETRIEBSGES.M.B.H._SEVERIN_WURNIG

hours-long beauty regime, and the deep-blue silk damask **Imperial Bedroom** (9). The dazzling white and gilt **Hall of Mirrors** (16) is where the six-year-old Mozart is said to have enraptured Maria Theresia during a performance in 1762.

But it's the palace centrum and Maria Theresia's apartments (rooms 19–40) that unveil some of the finest examples of rococo art. The visual apex is the 10m-wide ball and banquet room of the **Great Gallery** (21) with its crystal-glass mirror, stucco work and ceiling frescoes. It was the prestigious venue for the Congress of Vienna in 1814–15, reshaping Europe in the Napoleonic aftermath.

Next move to the **Oval Chinese Cabinet** (24), where exquisite gold-dissolved, black-lacquered panels stand out on white panelled walls. The **Blue Chinese Salon** (28), covered in 18th-century rice-paper wall hangings, is where the

TICKET OPTIONS
Vienna's most visited attraction has a bewildering array of ticket options. Skip the line and book before you arrive. If in doubt, the **Classic Pass** *(adult/child incl audio guide €40/31)* covers the main highlights.

QUICK BREAK
Enjoy a drink with a view to the palace at **Café Gloriette**, or sample the signature *Tafelspitz* – Emperor Franz Joseph I's favourite dish of prime boiled beef – at Viennese institution **Plachutta Stammhaus Hietzing**.

1918 renunciation of Emperor Karl I ended the Austro-Hungarian monarchy. Phenomenal gilded black lacquer cloaks the **Vieux Laque Room** (29), Maria Theresia's memorial room to her husband, Emperor Franz I Stephan of Lorraine.

The **Napoleon Room** (30) was the operational quarters of the French commander in Schloss Schönbrunn during his occupations of Vienna in 1805 and 1809. Be bamboozled in the **Porcelain Room** (31), whose three-dimensional garlands and frames are wood-made ceramic imitations. The priceless **Millions Room** (32) is embellished with rare rosewood panelling, while the ceremonial state bed remains preserved in a humidity-controlled chamber in the red velvet and gold embroidery swathed **Rich Room** (37).

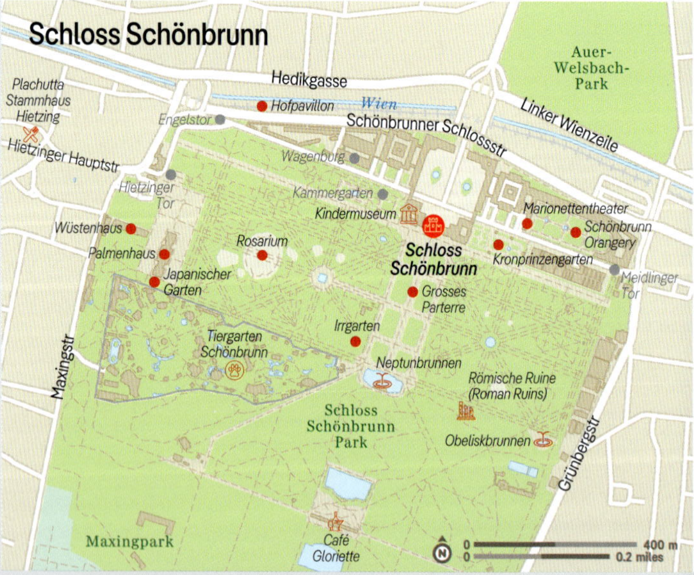

Schloss Schönbrunn

Auer-Welsbach-Park

Plachutta Stammhaus Hietzing

Hedikgasse

Wien

Schönbrunner Schlossstr

Linker Wienzeile

Engelstor

Hofpavillon

Hietzinger Hauptstr.

Wagenburg

Hietzinger Tor

Kammergarten

Marionettentheater

Wüstenhaus

Kindermuseum

Schloss Schönbrunn

Schönbrunn Orangery

Rosarium

Kronprinzengarten

Meidlinger Tor

Palmenhaus

Japanischer Garten

Grosses Parterre

Maxingstr

Tiergarten Schönbrunn

Irrgarten

Neptunbrunnen

Römische Ruine (Roman Ruins)

Schloss Schönbrunn Park

Obeliskbrunnen

Grünbergstr

Maxingpark

Café Gloriette

0   400 m
0   0.2 miles

A separate guided tour ticket *(adult/child €39/29)* is required for entrance to Maria Theresia's most precious ground-floor chambers – the exquisite mural-adorned **Bergl Rooms**. The tour continues through rooms 19–40.

Public Schönbrunn Park

Outside the regal digs is the square kilometre expanse of **Schloss Schönbrunn Park**, stretching from the **Grosses Parterre** (Great Parterre) symmetrical horticultural gardens to the Schönbrunn hill and cresting at the triumphant arch of the Gloriette. It opened to the public in 1779 and remains a city sanctuary for ramblers and runners and a drawing card for visitors wanting to wander the historical and cultural enclosure.

Notable features are the lavish palatial toppers by early classicist architect Johann Ferdinand Hetzendorf von Hohenberg, commissioned by Maria Theresia. These include the centrepiece **Neptunbrunnen** (Neptune Fountain; 1780) with its marbled staging of Neptune and his entourage being pulled across the seas; the **Obeliskbrunnen** (Obelisk Fountain; 1777), adorned with river gods and a golden-sphere-topped obelisk; and the crumbling colonnade archway of the **Römische Ruine** (Roman Ruins; 1778; pictured p131), an effigy of the ancient Roman temple of Vespasian and Titus. On the other side, the tranquil spaces of the **Rosarium** (Rose Garden) and **Japanischer Garten** (Japanese Garden) are backed by the enclosed Schönbrunn Zoo.

Garden Attractions

Ticketed entry allows access to unique attractions like the multi-climatic-zoned **Palmenhaus** (Palm House; *adult/child €9/7*) and the former imperial succulent-growing hothouse **Wüstenhaus** (Desert House; *adult/child €9/7*), which is now a re-created exhibition, including desert animals.

The secluded Privy Garden **Kronprinzengarten** (Crown Prince Garden) is a highlight; its elevated

40 ROOMS, TWO ROUTES

The 40 halls of state apartments and imperial chambers are accessible on two audio-guided routes with varying access. The 25-minute **State Apartments tour** *(adult/child €25/16)* covers central rooms 19–26, including the Great Gallery. The one-hour **Palace Ticket** *(€34/24)* encompasses all 40; the best value tour, it includes the private apartments of Emperor Franz Joseph and Empress Elisabeth and the sumptuous bundle of Maria Theresia's apartments.

GLORIETTE VIEWPOINT

The crowning viewpoint of Schönbrunn is upon the eagle-capped, arcaded archway of the **Gloriette**, added in 1775 on Schönbrunn hill. While the glass base houses Café Gloriette (p132), climbing to its balustrade roof provides commanding views of the palace with the sweep of Vienna rising above it in the background. You need a ticket to enter.

Garden on the Cellar parterre from around 1700 is wrapped with a tunnelled, trellised pergola, with a halfway viewing platform. The vaulted longhouse of the **Schönbrunn Orangery** details its 1754 beginnings when it was built as a temperature-controlled environment for the overwintering of citrus trees and the stage for grand banquets. Measuring 189m by 10m, it remains one of the two largest baroque orangeries in the world, alongside Versailles, and still grows exotic fruits.

The modern reconstruction of the original **Irrgarten** (Maze) from 1720 is a 2700-sq-metre circuit. It splits into a dead-end-dotted labyrinth that leads to a viewing platform and a 10-minute strolling course with mirrored and musical interactive stations.

If not purchasing a Classic Pass, the **Exclusive Gardens at Schönbrunn** *(adult/child €15/10)* combo ticket includes entrance to the Privy and Orangery gardens, the Maze (pictured right) and the Gloriette terrace.

Schönbrunn for Kids

Tiergarten Schönbrunn (Schönbrunn Zoo; *zoo vienna.at; adult/child €27/15.50*) is the oldest zoo in the world, founded in 1752 by Maria Theresia's husband, Emperor Franz I Stephan of Lorraine. Among its 500 species housed across 17 hectares are pandas, polar bears, tigers, rhinos, capybaras and more. A centre for international conservation research and breeding programmes, you can see some of the world's most endangered species here. Feedings typically take place every 30 minutes between 10am and 4pm.

Schönbrunn's **Kindermuseum** *(kindermuseum schoenbrunn.at; adult/child €12/12)* is a Habsburg-inspired playhouse where children can dress up as princes and princesses, and experience the life of little imperials through hands-on activities like setting the dinner table. Entry is by timed ticket.

The small **Marionettentheater** (Marionette Theatre) puts on majestic puppet performances

© SCHLOSS_SCHOENBRUNN_KULTUR-_UND_BETRIEBSGES.M.B.H._SEVERIN_WURNIG

of timeless operas like Mozart's *The Magic Flute*, continuing the centuries-old tradition using handcrafted wooden figures adorned in elaborate costumes. Most performances are in German.

The Summer Night Concert

Tickets for the worldwide broadcast of the Wiener Philharmoniker (Vienna Philharmonic) New Year's Concert are like gold dust, but if you find yourself in Vienna in June, you'll catch the mid-year classical-music highlight. The **Summer Night Concert** (*wienerphilharmoniker.at*) at Schloss Schönbrunn is a free open-air show staged on the baroque lawn between the iconic palace and its elevated Gloriette monument. If you can't snag a chair in front of the orchestra podium, join the tens of thousands of locals setting down a blanket on the slopes.

EXPERIENCES

Admire the Imperial Railway Pavilion

ARCHITECTURE

MAP: **1** P128 **E2**

If you're travelling to Schönbrunn Palace by metro, don't miss the **Hofpavillon** (Imperial Pavilion; *wienmuseum.at/otto_wagner _hofpavillon_hietzing; adult/child €5/free*) at the end of Hietzing Station. Designed by Otto Wagner, the mahogany octagonal waiting salon was Emperor Franz Joseph's private access to the metropolitan railway, although he only used it twice.

Walk in the Biosphere Park

NATURE RESERVE

MAP: **2** P128 **A5**

Covering almost half of Hietzing is the former imperial hunting ground turned 25-sq-km public nature reserve and protected biosphere park, **Lainzer Tiergarten** (Lainzer Zoo). Around 80% is a forest and meadow habitat harbouring a zoological and botanical intermix, including 400-year-old beech and oak trees, nearly 100 bird species, and stag and boar among its wild residents. The park's longer marked trails are better suited to experienced walkers. For an introduction, head on a 40-minute signposted track above Hermesvilla to the elevated Wienerblick vantage point. Exit at St Veiter Tor, and take bus 54A or B from Ghelengasse/Stock im Weg to the Hietzing U-Bahn. Note that gates can close as early as 5pm in winter.

Step Inside Sisi's Summer Retreat

VILLA

MAP: **3** P128 **A5**

Empress Elisabeth's verdant-set summer palace **Hermesvilla** (*wienmuseum.at/hermesvilla; adult/child €8/free*) was created by the architect of the Naturhistorisches and Kunsthistorisches Museums, Karl von Hasenauer, at the request of the Emperor Franz Joseph. The private imperial getaway's pièce de résistance is Elisabeth's bedroom with artwork by Austrian painters Franz Matsch, Hugo Charlemont, Gustav Klimt and his brother Ernst, each adding their brushstroke to the *A Midsummer Night's Dream* murals. Guided tours and exhibits are in German only. Access is from Lainzer Tiergarten's Lainzer Tor entrance.

See Klimt's Final Studio

EXHIBITION

MAP: **4** P128 **A2**

The two-storey neo-baroque **Klimt Villa** (*klimtvilla.at; adult/child €10/free*) in residential Hietzing isn't the exact property he lived in – it was extended by the owners some five years after his death. Yet the renovations in 2012 saw the original ground floor of the summer house restored, preserving Gustav's reception room and final studio space where he worked on 50 paintings between 1911 and his death in 1918. A permanent exhibition focuses on the Klimt works lost and stolen.

LISTINGS

Best Places for...

€ Budget €€ Midrange €€€ Top End

Eating
International
Waldemar-Tagesbar €€

 5 B6

Casual, stylish cafe-bar with a sizeable breakfast menu and brunch cocktails, sandwiches, smoothies and barista coffee. *8am-10pm Mon-Fri, 9am-3pm Sat & Sun*

Nook €€

6 B6

This earthy-minimalist style cafe offers a guaranteed hip platter of speciality coffee, sourdough bread and house-baked pastries and cakes. *9am-6pm Mon-Sun*

Vegan & Vegetarian
Hollerei €€

 7 H3

Art-splashed tavern with terraced garden serving vegan and vegetarian dishes. It's in the neighbouring 15th district, close to the Schönbrunn U-Bahn. *11am-11pm Mon-Sat*

Drinking
Cafes
Café Dommayer

 8 B5

Hietzing's legacy red banquette and chandeliered coffee house is a traditional mainstay and serves pastries and cakes from Viennese confectioner Oberlaa. *7.30am-8.30pm*

Bars & Beer Halls
Gloriette Bar im Parkhotel Schönbrunn

9 C5

The grand building beside the park is the restored guesthouse of Emperor Franz Joseph. In today's hotel bar, sip in the chandeliered salon with views into Schönbrunn. *5pm-1am Tue-Sat*

Brandauer Schlossbräu

 10 C6

This historic beer hall holds an imperial-era dining room and huge garden terrace

See p128 for map of locations

EXPLORE

SCHLOSS SCHÖNBRUNN: HIETZING

beyond its unassuming entrance. A hearty menu accompanies the house Zwickl and Helles beer. *10am-midnight*

Shopping
Lifestyle
Travel UPGRADE

 11 B6

Travel gear concept store stocking only sustainable brand luggage, accessories and toiletries. Also has a selection of games, guides and coffee books. *10am-6pm Mon-Fri, to 3pm Sat*

Vintage
Nuk13

12 B6

The sister outlet of Nook opened a cool closet opposite – a trove of handpicked, secondhand vintage wears. It's cubby cafe corner offers coffee and cookies. *10am-5.30pm Thu-Sun*

★ WORTH A TRIP

The Wachau Valley

Bike, hike, rail or cruise along the Danube River between medieval Krems and baroque abbey-topped Melk – the two gateways to the medieval hamlets and terraced vineyards of the Wachau Valley – passing pastel-hued Dürnstein and the idyllic village of Spitz on the way.

PLANNING TIP
The fastest train to Krems (65 minutes) is the REX 4 service; to Melk, the CJX 5 (63 minutes). Both depart hourly from Vienna's Franz-Josefs-Bahnhof (9th district).

Bike the Danube Cycle Path

Stage 5 of the long-distance **Danube Cycle Path** passes through the Wachau Valley for some 35km. Hire a bike at **Wachau Explorer** (*wachauexplorer.at*) in Krems, hop on the train to Emmersdorf or the boat to Melk, then cycle back. Tracing the Danube's north bank on two wheels, you'll pass the Aggstein Castle ruins in Aggsbach Markt, see the home of the famed Palaeolithic figurine *Venus of Willendorf,* break in the scenic market town of Spitz, view Weissenkirchen's fortified 14th-century gothic church, clamber the ruins of **Dürnstein Castle** where Richard the Lionheart was held captive in the winter of 1192, and finish back in the 1000-year-old wine town of Krems. Shorten the journey by starting in Spitz.

Hike the Wachau World Heritage Trail

The **Wachau World Heritage Trail** spans 14 routes; **Trail 1** (12.4km; 4½ hours) connects Krems to Dürnstein, passing a patchwork of stone terraced vineyards, forests and undulating hills with Danube views. Dürnstein, with its medieval streets, baroque facades and porcelain-blue abbey tower, is the picture-perfect stop. From here, take the train back to Krems. In April, the Wachau Marille (apricot) will be in bloom. Just as famed as its wine, the prized apricot features on every menu in many forms, from cakes to schnapps.

Scan this QR code for Danube Cycle Path and Wachau World Heritage Trail routes.

KOCHNEVA TETYANA/SHUTTERSTOCK

The Wachau by River & Rail

For a tranquil journey along the Wachau's emerald valley, take a cruise along the Danube or trundle through on the panoramic Wachau Rail.

DDSG Blue Danube Cruises (*ddsg-blue-danube.at/cruises-wachau; single/return €39/47, bikes adult/child €3/1.50*) depart from Krems and Melk up to four times a day between April and November – a one-way journey takes just under two hours passing the wine-growing towns of Dürnstein, Weissenkirchen, Spitz and Emmersdorf, with elevated views across the river to Melk. If you want to spend time on land, there are shorter trips between towns, with departures to and from Spitz and Dürnstein.

The **Wachau Bahn** (Wachau Railway; *wachaubahn.at*) has been charting a route through the valley for over 100 years between Krems and Emmersdorf (*adult/child single €20/9.50, return €27/12.50, bikes free*). It runs March to November.

QUICK BREAK
In Dürnstein, stop for wine tasting at the renowned **Domäne Wachau** (*domaene-wachau.at*) estate, or enjoy a riverside afternoon tea at the **Hotel Schloss Dürnstein** (*schloss.at*).

Vienna Toolkit

Graben (p55)
MOLARJUNG/SHUTTERSTOCK

Family Travel

Vienna is a wonder-filled and welcoming place for kids of all ages, packing in palaces and gardens, parks and playgrounds, a zoo, aquarium and amusement fair, multimedia museums and dedicated exhibition spaces.

Vienna Is Great for Kids

Austrian culture generally encourages learning and time spent in the great outdoors. In Vienna, while dining establishments welcome children, it's museums that typically go out of their way to cater to them. Public parks are family-centric; most have a play area or enough space to burn off energy.

Eating Out

You'll rarely find a dedicated children's menu, but smaller portions can be arranged. Kids' facilities in establishments are rare, though many have high-chairs. Spaces geared for young ones include the MuseumsQuartier's youth theatre hangout, **Dschungel Café** and the 2nd district's **Family & Friends** restaurant. Prater's **Rollercoaster Restaurant** and the 4th district's **Výtopna Railway Restaurant** deliver drinks and meals on tracks.

FAMILY-FRIENDLY STAYS

The capital's hotels are family-friendly. Cots and extra beds are available, and at many hotels, children under three years old stay for free, and those under 12 often receive discounts. Others offer cuddly toys and kids' amenities.

Sunday Special

On the first Sunday of every month, many museums offer free admission to everyone, regardless of age.

Public Transport

Free for children under six years; half-price fare on single tickets for under 15 years.

Admission Fees

Many top museums, including the Naturhistorisches Museum (p50), Belvedere (p86) and Albertina (p42), offer free entry to visitors under 19 years old. Others provide discounts and family ticket deals, or free entry for children under six.

Accommodation

From luxurious historic palaces and boutique art hotels to eco-friendly stays and trendy hostels – Vienna caters to every style and budget.

Where to Stay if You Love...

 ### History, Architecture & Museums
1st district, Innere Stadt (p35) Vienna's centre has everything from modest pensions to heritage hotels on the doorstep of historic sites.

OUR PICK

⭐

We Love to Stay in the...
7th district, Neubau (p111). This creative neighbourhood borders the historic centre but is far from touristy, spilling out around the MuseumsQuartier and filling a grid of hip laneways with vintage and vinyl stores, craft bars and cocktail joints. You can be at big-hitter sights within a 30-minute walk or reach other points of interest with an easy U-Bahn ride.

Luxury Living
Ringstrasse (p56) Many of the former noble residences on this architectural belt road are now the city's most sumptuous hotels.

HOW MUCH FOR A NIGHT IN A

Hostel dorm bed **from €30**

Trendy midrange hotel **from €100**

High-end central hotel **from €300**

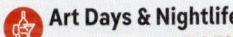

 ### Art Days & Nightlife
6th district, Mariahilf (p97) The core of downtown's late-night hangouts, within a 20-minute walk to the major art museums.

Trendy Neighbourhoods
2nd district, Leopoldstadt (p69) Vienna's hippest neighbourhood spreads from the gritty Danube Canal, a U-Bahn stop (or two) to the centre.

 ### Residential Peace & Quiet
3rd district, Landstrasse (p83) The quiet residential wedge behind Stadtpark is only a 25-minute walk from the historic centre.

143

Food, Drink & Nightlife

⚠ Allergies & Intolerances

Those with allergies and intolerances should have no issues when eating out in Vienna. Most menus include letters indicating the presence of potential allergen ingredients, such as Grain (A), Egg (C), Milk or Lactose (G), Fish (D), Peanut (E) and Soy (F). However, it's always best to ask and be sure.

HOW TO SAY

I'm allergic to... Ich bin allergisch gegen...
Nuts Nüsse
Seafood Meeresfrüchte
Dairy products Milchproduckte
Gluten Gluten

❓ HOW TO ASK...

Is this gluten free?
Ist das glutenfrei?
Does this contain nuts?
Enthält das Nüsse?
Is there a vegan option? / Is there anything for vegans?
Gibt es etwas für Veganer?

MEAT-FREE METROPOLIS

Meat-free and plant-based options are plentiful. Restaurants typically have a small vegetarian offering, but specialist restaurants are flourishing; **Tian Bistro am Spittelberg** (p124) and **Donnersmarkt** focus on seasonal and experimental fare. **Veggiezz**, **Swing Kitchen** and **Plain Vienna** are great for healthy fast food bites.

🏪 Markt Life

Markets are a way of life in Vienna, whose fresh produce and sample-laden stalls are usually neighboured with bars and restaurants. The largest markets in the city are **Naschmarkt** (p107) with 120 food stalls and **Brunnenmarkt** (p121) with a multicultural mix of 170 vendors. Or opt for tasty bites at **Karmelitermarkt** (p79) or the delicacy-stacked **Kutschkermarkt**.

HOW TO... Pay the Bill

Unless the server needs to cash up, you won't be presented with your bill. Politely catch the server's attention and say: *'Die Rechnung, bitte'* or *'Zahlen, bitte'*.

Payment
Servers will typically ask *'Mit Karte oder Bargeld?'* (with card or cash?) and *'Zusammen oder getrennt?'* (together or separate?) Splitting the bill is no problem; the server will cash up individually or split the bill evenly.

Tipping
Tipping is not usually included in the bill. In restaurants, 10% is standard; in cafes and bars, round up to the nearest euro or two. Specify the total amount you wish to pay (including the tip). *'Stimmt so'* means keep the change.

PRICE RANGES

The following price ranges refer to the cost for a two-course meal:

€ less than €15
€€ €15–30
€€€ more than €30

OPENING HOURS

Cafes 8am–11pm
Restaurants 11am–11pm (many offer special lunch menus)
Würstelstand noon–3am

 Going Out

Club scene While Vienna isn't famous for club culture, there's a choice of electronic and techno music clubs such as **Flex**, **Fluc**, **Donau** and **Grelle Forelle**. For a bridge between genres, **Volksgarten Club Disco** is a historic institution in the Hofburg's garden, while former Art Deco-era relic **Cabaret Fledermaus** hosts themed music nights.

Bar scene The capital's drinking scene is laid-back and informal. Popular hangouts are the poster-clad, youthful *Beisln* (bistro-pubs), like **Atlas** (p125), and the alternative and live music joints that fill the railway arches along the Gürtel road, including **Chelsea** (p121) and **Café Carina** (p121). Low-key, experimental cocktail bars like **Die Parfümerie** (p125) are popular, while the most creative, such as **Plus43** (p125), are often hidden.

When to go Bars can open anytime from 4–6pm and close around 2am. Clubs can stay thumping until 6am.

NEW AFRICA/SHUTTERSTOCK

HOW MUCH FOR A

Coffee
€6

Sacher Torte (chocolate and apricot cake)
€10.50

Kaiserschmarrn (sweet pancake)
€12.90

Wiener Schnitzel
€20

Gulasch (thick stew)
€16

Käsekrainer (smoked sausage)
€6

Glass of wine
€4

Pint of beer
€5

LGBTIQ+ Travellers

Although historically conservative, Vienna has become increasingly open and embracing of diversity and is today home to a lively LGBTIQ+ scene.

LGBTIQ+ Scene

Vienna doesn't have a single stand-out 'gayborhood', but you'll find the LGBTIQ+ community centred around Naschmarkt in the Wieden (4th) and Mariahilf (6th) districts. The city's largest concentration of queer-owned establishments and bars has grown around the historic market-side **Türkis Rosa Lila Villa** refuge and its queer community institution, **Villa Vida** cafe.

The city is broadly queer-friendly; everywhere from bars and bookstores to cultural spaces and clubs promotes inclusivity. In the neighbouring artistic and creative district of Neubau (7th), Vienna's oldest LGBTIQ+ bar, Mango Bar, has opened a queer rooftop bar in the MuseumsQuartier, while the 80s-opened **Why Not Queer** remains a mainstay in the Innere Stadt (1st).

NITO/SHUTTERSTOCK

PRIDE

Every June, the Ringstrasse is filled with tune-pumping floats for Vienna's Pride event, the **Regenbogen Parade** (Rainbow Parade) – the city's biggest annual LGBTIQ+ celebration.

QUEER VIENNA LOCATIONS

Vienna Tourism's **ivie app** pinpoints the 'Rainbow Capital' highlights on a self-guided tour of legendary LGBTIQ+ locations.

Resources

● **Türkis Rosa Lila Villa** (Die Villa; *dievilla.at*) The historic safe house has information on what's on offer in Vienna. ● **HOSI** *(hosiwien.at)* Advocate group hosting events at their community centre, Das Gugg. ● **Vienna Tourism** *(wien.info/en/vienna-for/gay -lesbian)* Has city-wide event listings.

Health & Safe Travel

Vienna is one of the safest cities in the world, but it always pays to be aware and take precautions.

TAP WATER

Leitungswasser (tap water) is sourced from the Lower Austrian-Styrian Alps, making it safe to drink, whether you fill up from the hotel or the city's drinking fountains. Cafes and restaurants will serve tap water, although *Mineralwasser* (sparkling water) is also a popular choice.

Chemist vs Pharmacy

Drogerien (chemist stores) such as DM, Bipa and Müller don't sell any kind of medication, but are helpful for basic first aid supplies. Over-the-counter medicines, including basic painkillers like paracetamol, are only available at *Apotheken* (pharmacies) and will likely cost more than what you pay at home. Alongside your regular medications, pack pills for allergies, aches and pains. *Apotheken* display in their window if they offer an after-hours service, or call 1455 or check *nachtapotheke.wien*.

Transport
Not just driving, but biking while inebriated is a punishable offence (usually a hefty fine).

Health Insurance

Free or reduced-cost state-provided healthcare and emergency medical treatment are available in Vienna for citizens from EU countries, Switzerland, Liechtenstein, Norway, Iceland and the UK with a valid European Health Insurance Card (EHIC). Any costs incurred are paid and reimbursed by your national insurer upon return; private healthcare treatments and repatriation costs are not covered. Consider comprehensive travel insurance for full medical coverage.

CASH MACHINES

Avoid inflated cash withdrawal surcharges at independent ATMs like Euronet; withdraw from an Austrian Bankomat displaying blue and green stripes, including Erste, Raiffeisen and Bank Austria.

QUICK INFO

Vaccinations
Consider the tick-borne encephalitis (TBE) vaccination if you plan to visit forested areas.

Theft
Petty crime, like pick-pocketing, can occur in tourist areas like Stephansplatz.

Marijuana
Buying, possessing or consuming cannabis for recreational use remains illegal.

Responsible Travel

Vienna champions sustainable initiatives. Follow these tips to leave a lighter footprint, support local businesses and have a positive impact on communities.

Give Back

Vienna's social democratic heritage is rooted in community development, with businesses actively addressing social issues. **magdas HOTEL**, Austria's first social business hotel, trains refugees and migrants, while **Habibi & Hawara** is the capital's first restaurant run by refugees. Generational cafe **Vollpension** serves coffee and cake with 'Oma and Opa' hosts, while **Shades Tours** city walks are led by individuals affected by homelessness and addiction, rebuilding their lives as guides.

Local Souvenirs

Skip mass-produced souvenirs and choose Viennese-crafted Augarten porcelain, *Heuriger* wine glasses, Original Viennese Snow Globes and iconic Manner wafers. Shop design-led trinkets at **World to Go Vienna** and **Hamtil & Söhne** stores.

FROM LEFT: FLORIAN WIESER/EPA-EFE/SHUTTERSTOCK, NEW AFRICA/SHUTTERSTOCK

OUR PICK

⭐

No Waste Eats
Hotels, bakeries and restaurants fight food waste by selling discounted unsold food through the **Too Good to Go app** (toogoodtogo.com/de-at).

Green City

It may be an architecturally wondrous metropolis, but Vienna is no concrete jungle. The public grounds of Augarten and Stadtpark, the landscaped Schönbrunn and Belvedere gardens and the lawns of Volksgarten; the meadow stretch of Prater and the biosphere Lainzer Tiergarten; the Vienna woods and city vineyards – half of Vienna is green space, and 14 city hiking trails forge paths through it all.

Scan this QR code to find a walking trail

Resources

● **Umweltzeichen.at** Lists Austrian Ecolabel-certified stays, dining and tourism spaces. ● **smartcity.wien.gv.at/en/strategy** Details the city's climate strategy and urban initiatives.

OVERTOURISM

Visit during the low and shoulder seasons (March to May and September to November) and help ease the strain at popular sites. Stay longer than two days and explore beyond the Innere Stadt, museums and landmarks.

Sustainable Stays

Vienna tightened regulations on short-term rental properties in residential areas, so give the city a hand and avoid them. There are numerous eco-minded and socially conscious hotels and accommodations, many of which have been awarded the Austrian Ecolabel. The noise-reducing and air-purifying green facade of **Hotel Gilbert** is also a bird home, while **Hotel Daniel**, **25hours Hotel Wien** and **Hotel InterContinental** host rooftop beehives. **Boutiquehotel Stadthalle** operates with a 'zero energy balance' using photovoltaic solar power on its lavender garden roof. Others like **Magdas** and **Superbude** put upcycling at the core of their design.

DRINKING FOUNTAINS

Reduce plastic waste by bringing a reusable water bottle. The city's 1300 drinking fountains (and cooling water mist sprays) bring fresh mountain water from the Lower Austrian-Styrian Alps to the streets.

Climate Change & Travel

It's impossible to ignore the impact we have when travelling; Lonely Planet urges all travellers to engage with their travel carbon footprint, which will mainly come from air travel. While there often isn't an alternative, travellers can look to minimise the number of flights they take, opt for newer aircraft and use cleaner ground transport, such as trains. One proposed solution – purchasing carbon offsets – unfortunately does not cancel out the impact of individual flights. While most destinations will depend on air travel for the foreseeable future, for now, pursuing ground-based travel where possible is the best course of action.

The **UN Carbon Offset Calculator** shows how flying impacts a household's emissions.

The **ICAO's carbon emissions calculator** allows visitors to analyse the CO_2 generated by point-to-point journeys.

Accessible Travel

Transport

All U-Bahn stations and trains have wheelchair access and guiding strips for the blind. All buses have folding ramps. The majority of trams (indicated by a wheelchair symbol on the electronic display) have low-floor access allowing wheelchair entry. Traffic lights make a 'tack, tack' sound to indicate when it's safe for pedestrians to cross the road.

Museums

All major museums, including the Naturhistorisches and Kunsthistorisches Museums, Leopold, Belvedere and Schönbrunn, have ramp or side entrances, lifts, barrier-free toilets and wheelchair rental. Audio guides are available, and guided tours for the blind and visually impaired can be booked in advance.

OUR PICK

The **Kunsthistorisches Museum** (p46) offers blind and visually impaired visitors a unique opportunity to experience the museum and three Renaissance art masterpieces from its Picture Gallery on a touch-focused tour. Going beyond Braille brochures, the guided tour utilises foils, 3D reliefs and other materials in a tactile exploration that includes Raphael's *Madonna in Green*, Albrecht Dürer's *Madonna and Child* and Jean Fouquet's *Gonella, the Ferrara Court Jester*. Registration is required for participation.

ACCOMMODATION

Hotels with accessible facilities are plentiful. Larger capacity hotels can have up to five adapted rooms, while smaller properties may only have one. Lifts are common, though historic properties may have long corridors and heavy doors.

Bicycle Taxis

For those who tire easily from walking, you can grab one of the rickshaws that trundle around the city. Bicycle taxi service **Faxi** *(faxi .at/barrierefrei)* offers wheelchair-accessible bikes and tailor-made city tours.

COBBLESTONES

Vienna's cobblestoned streets are mostly confined to the historic centre. Though uneven surfaces are not ideal for wheelchair users, paved roads and sidewalks still make much of the Innere Stadt accessible.

Resources

● **wien.info/en/travel-info/accessible-vienna** Vienna Tourism's detailed accessibility guide provides information on establishments with disabled access, medical facilities, parking places, toilets and more.

Nuts & Bolts

Opening Hours

Many hospitality establishments and entertainment venues remain open on holidays, though some shut shop in July/August.

Coffeehouses 8am–11pm

Restaurants 11am–11pm

Bars 6pm–1am

Pubs 4pm–2am

Clubs 10pm–6am

Shops 10am–6pm; some high-street stores have late opening on Thursday and Friday until 8pm; Saturday early closure at 5pm. All close on Sunday.

Supermarkets 8am–8pm Monday–Friday; Saturday until 6pm; all close on Sunday.

Banks From 8/9am; closing hours vary. All major banks have street-access ATMs.

Toilets

Washrooms at U-Bahn and train stations, as well as some public 'WC' facilities, incur a €0.50 charge. Shopping centres and department stores have free-to-use facilities. Museums reliably have good, clean toilets. At cafes and bars, bathrooms are only for paying customers; ask first or purchase a coffee.

ELECTRICITY
Type F 230V/50Hz

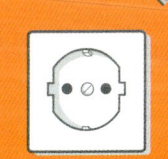

Public Holidays

Museums typically remain open, closing only for Christmas Day and New Year's Day.

New Year's Day 1 January

Epiphany 6 January

Easter Monday March or April

Labour Day 1 May

Ascension Day Sixth Thursday after Easter

Whit Monday Sixth Monday after Easter

Corpus Christi Second Thursday after Pentecost

Assumption 15 August

National Day 26 October

All Saints' Day 1 November

Immaculate Conception 8 December

Christmas Eve 24 December; afternoon closures

Christmas Day 25 December

St Stephen's Day 26 December

Language

German Basics

Hello.
Grüss Gott.
grewss-got
Servus. *ser*-vus

Goodbye.
Auf Wiedersehen.
owf *vee*-der-zay-en

Yes.
Ja. yah

No.
Nein. nain

Please.
Bitte. *bi*-te

Thank you.
Danke. *dang*-ke

Excuse me/Sorry.
Entschuldigung.
ent-*shul*-di-gung

You're welcome.
Bitte. *bi*-te

Fast Phrases

What's your name?
Wie ist Ihr Name? (pol) vee ist eer *nah*·me
Wie heißt du? (inf) vee haist doo

My name is ...
Mein Name ist ... (pol) main *nah*·me ist ...
Ich heiße ... (inf) ikh hai·se ...

Do you speak English?
Sprechen Sie Englisch? *shpre*·khen zee *eng*·lish

I don't understand.
Ich verstehe nicht. ikh fer·*shtay*·e nikht

What time is it? Wie spät ist es? vee shpayt ist es
It's (10) o'clock. Es ist (zehn) Uhr. es ist (tsayn) oor
morning Morgen *mor*·gen
afternoon Nachmittag *nahkh*·mi·tahk
evening Abend *ah*·bent
yesterday gestern *ges*·tern
today heute *hoy*·te
tomorrow morgen *mor*·gen

Where's (the station)?
Wo ist (der Bahnhof). vo ist (der *bahn*·hawf)

Could you please write it down?
Könnten Sie das bitte aufschreiben? *kern*·ten zee das *bi*·te *owf*·shrai·ben

Can you show me (on the map)?
Können Sie es mir (auf der Karte) zeigen *ker*·nen zee es meer (owf dair *kar*·te) *tsai*·gen

Numbers

 eins *ains*

 zwei *tsvai*

 drei *drai*

 vier *feer*

 fünf *fünf*

Eszett & the Umlauts

In German, the ß character is called *eszett*. Look out for it in words like *Straße*, meaning street. It's often transliterated as 'ss' (which is used in this book).

The two dots that sometimes appear above the vowels a, o and u are called *umlauts* and affect how words are pronounced. You'll see them in words like *Bäckerei* (bakery), *Löffel* (spoon) and *Frühstück* (breakfast).

Formalities

German has a formal and informal word for 'you' (*Sie* zee and *du* doo respectively). When talking to someone familiar or younger than you, use the informal *du* form.

Signs

Ausgang Exit
Eingang Entrance
Damen Women
Herren Men
Heiß Hot
Kalt Cold
Offen Open
Geschlossen Closed
Kein Zutritt No Entry
Rauchen Verboten
No Smoking
Verboten Prohibited
Toiletten (WC) Toilets
Flughafen Airport
Zieken Pull
Drucken Push

EMERGENCIES

Help! Hilfe! *hil*·fe
Go away! Gehen Sie weg! *gay*·en zee vek
I'm ill. Ich bin krank. ikh bin krangk
Call the police! Rufen Sie die Polizei! *roo*·fen zee dee po·li·*tsai*
Call a doctor! Rufen Sie einen Arzt! *roo*·fen zee *ai*·nen artst

Must-Know Sounds

Note that **kh** sounds like the 'ch' in 'Bach' or in the Scottish loch (pronounced at the back of the throat), **r** is also pronounced at the back of the throat, and **ü** as the 'ee' in 'see' but with rounded lips.

— FALSE FRIENDS —

Warning: many German words look like English words but have a different meaning altogether, eg *Chef* shef is boss, not chef (which is *Koch* in German). *Tipp* tip is 'advance information' (not 'bonus payment', which is *Trinkgeld* trink·gelt); *komisch* kaw·mish is 'strange' (not 'comical', which is *lustig* lus·tikh); and *blank* blank is 'shiny' (not 'blank', which is *leer* leer).

6 **sechs** *zeks*

7 **sieben** *zee·ben*

8 **acht** *akht*

9 **neun** *noyn*

10 **zehn** *tsayn*

Index

Sights p000   Map pages p000

See also separate subindexes for:

 Eating p157

 Drinking p158

🛍 **Shopping p159**

INDEX

154

 **Eating**

Drinking

Send Us Your Feedback

We love to hear from travellers – your comments help make our books better. We read every word, and we guarantee that your feedback goes straight to the authors. Visit lonelyplanet.com/contact to submit your updates and suggestions.

Note: We may edit, reproduce and incorporate your comments in Lonely Planet products such as guidebooks, websites and digital products, so let us know if you are happy to have your name acknowledged. For a copy of our privacy policy visit lonelyplanet.com/legal.

Acknowledgements

Cover photograph: The Pestsäule (Plague Column; p55). Jorg Greuel/Getty Images

Back photograph: Prater Park (p72). BABAROGA/Shutterstock

THIS BOOK

The 6th edition of Lonely Planet's Vienna guidebook was researched and written by Becki Enright. The previous edition was also written by Becki. This guidebook was produced by the following:

Destination Editor
Sandie Kestell

Coordinating Editor
Gabrielle Innes

Cartographer
Julie Sheridan

Production Editor
Robin Yule

Image Editor
Lyn Horst

Cover Researchers
Gwen Cotter, Daisy Korpics

Thanks to
Sofie Andersen, Fergal Condon, Kellie Langdon, Wayne Murphy, Charlotte Orr, Saralinda Turner, Clifton Wilkinson

Although the authors and Lonely Planet have taken all reasonable care in preparing this book, we make no warranty about the accuracy or completeness of its content and, to the maximum extent permitted, disclaim all liability arising from its use.

Published by Lonely Planet Global Limited
CRN 554153
6th edition – Jun 2026
ISBN 978 1 83869 929 1
© Lonely Planet 2026
10 9 8 7 6 5 4 3 2 1
Printed in China

Shopping